D1487709

How to be Not Too Bad

HOW TO BE
NOT TOO BAD

A Canadian Guide to Superior Behaviour

With illustrations by Graham Pilsworth

Charles Gordon

CANADIAN CATALOGUING IN PUBLICATION DATA
Gordon, Charles, 1940-
How to be not too bad
ISBN 0-7710-3392-3
I. Pilsworth, Graham, 1944-.   II. Title.
PS8563.0632H69 1993   c817'.54   c93-093202-1
PR9199.3.G662H69 1993

Typesetting by M&S, Toronto
Printed and bound in Canada on acid-free paper

The publishers acknowledge the support of the Canada Council and the
Ontario Arts Council for their publishing program.
The support of the Government of Ontario through the Ministry of
Culture and Communications is acknowledged.

Parts of Chapter 3 ("How To Be A Cottage Guest" and" The Rules for
Cottage Hosts") have appeared in *Cottage Life*.

A Douglas Gibson Book
McClelland & Stewart Inc.
The Canadian Publishers
481 University Avenue
Toronto, Ontario
M5G 2E9

Contents

For the two best laughers in the world,
Mary G. and Mary P.

Chapter 1

Why This Book? Why You Ask?

The Trouble with the World Today

The pursuit of excellence isn't going too well and many of us are losing heart. Some of us are losing face too, and at this rate pretty soon there won't be much of us left. Before we begin losing foot, we have to readjust our sights. There is an arrogance in trying to be perfect, an unseemly haste in trying to be first. What we should be trying is to be not too bad – an achievable and entirely Canadian goal.

Not that it will be easy. There is so much to be confused about in this day and age, and the next day and age too. If you think the next day and age is going to be less confusing than this one, you don't know your days and ages.

You are basically a good person. You want to survive and you want to be ethical about it, if at all possible. Yet the array of moral choices broadens. There are events you are not even aware of now that you will be called upon to behave properly at; there are places you have never been, professions you didn't know existed, activities you had not imagined. There is a good chance that you will embarrass yourself if you do not get the right advice.

Think of this. When you were born, there was no such

thing as a video store. There was only a handful of social diseases. The concept of political correctness was in the future. There were no computer viruses. There were no computers, except for that big clunky thing that needed its own building over at the university. Relations between the sexes were simpler, at least as far as anyone knew. It may simply have been a matter of the more complicated types of human sexuality not getting as much publicity.

Now there are all these things. There are compact discs and the end of the Cold War. There are several dozen former Soviet republics, or so it seems. There is the designated hitter, the slam dunk; there are thirty-five channels in every home. There is bad cholesterol and good cholesterol. There are male strippers, animal rights advocates, surrogate mothers, prepaid funerals, driver's-side air bags, affirmative action, Chinese fortune cookies in English and French, free-standing abortion clinics, space shuttles, gold, silver, and bronze unleaded gasoline, cellular phones, and barbecue-flavour pita puffs. Nothing your mother told you could prepare you for any of this.

The world is rapidly changing and might soon pass us by. Some people think this is good. "What about we just let the world pass us by," they say. "Maybe something else will come along, a better world or something like that." But most of us want to stay in the world. Our major qualm is that staying in the world seems to take a lot out of us. What we need is a philosophy that will get us ready for the future at the same time as it helps us cope with the present. We need new etiquette, new manners – the whole nine yards, as Emily Post used to say.

Do we need new mores, or just more mores? It is hard to know. Can we change the world? Even if we wanted to, it would be hard to find anyone who had the time to help us do it. Everyone is so busy these days.

Of course, all this may pass. Sometimes it does. Disco

died. Stalin died. So there is something to be said for waiting it out. What we seek is a strategy that will help us do so, positively and creatively if at all possible.

But what of the future, eh? Well, first we must understand the present, because it contains the seeds of the future, as someone once said. It is just as true now as it ever was that we should not spit out the seeds. How all this fits into the global context will be made clearer when we examine our present world and make certain scientific predictions, and other kinds too.

The Trouble with the World Today

Many people in the developed world now take it as gospel that busy people don't have time to both condition and shampoo. This is a concept largely unknown in the underdeveloped world, where there is not as much television. Because of the way the developed world has developed, it views the deprivation of the underdeveloped world in terms of how few television channels it gets.

It is possible to ask why, given our unlimited access to television and given our attitude to shampooing and conditioning, we are still developed and the others still underdeveloped. The answer can only be that they are incredibly unlucky and that some day their luck will change. Then we will get all the typhoons, droughts, and floods and see how well we do.

One of the measures of our global ignorance is that we don't recognize it. That is because we live in the Information Age. In the Information Age, the sum total of our knowledge increases by 17½ per cent every eight days, although those may not be the correct figures. We now have available to us on a single compact disc information that once took six complete university library buildings to house, not counting washrooms and broom closets. All of that makes us think we are pretty smart.

Along with thinking we are pretty smart, we have lost our sense of wonder and don't have the sense to wonder where it went. There are no mysteries to us, because we have seen them all solved on television. Wild animals don't awe us; we have no automatic respect, any more, for people in uniforms, even milkmen. We have seen bad cops and bad politicians on television; we have seen bad clergymen on the evening news.

We don't dress up to travel any more. That is because we are not afraid of airplanes. In the first twenty or thirty years of air travel, men, women, and children showed up at the airport respectfully early, wearing their church clothes. Those people didn't understand airplanes, but they had an innate sense that airplanes were heavier than air and had no business flying. Only the pilots (and perhaps the stewardesses and perhaps the gods) could keep them up in the air, so there was no percentage in annoying them in any way, such as by arriving less than an hour early or going without a necktie. In retrospect, those were the golden days of air travel. Most people were afraid to fly. Others lacked the proper clothes for it. So airports were uncrowded, plane seats were wider, and kids could go sit with the pilot.

Now, in the Information Age, everybody knows how a plane flies, or can access the information in a jiff. The mystery is out of that. There is no reason to dress up for the pilot, and besides we've seen many bad pilots on TV. Airplanes are full of fat men in short shorts, wearing sandals and beer T-shirts. We live in an age of no respect for airplanes.

The Information Age has given us the computer, which enables us to be ruder and stupider at much greater speed and to many more people at a single time than at any other time in human history. With just a few keystrokes we can send insulting messages to thousands of people at the same time or tell them that their jobs have been taken away, moved to a non-union town, or handed over to robots. Another product of the computer technology, the credit card, enables us to go deeply into debt without leaving our homes, and to get in line for theatre tickets ahead of ordinary people without cards who stand outside the theatre in the cold. We know that little cards will have even greater power in the years to come, and and we know we have our work cut out for us, surviving happily in such a world.

That is ironic, in view of the fact that the world seems to have increased its own chances of survival. The Cold War has ended, a fact that should have made us breathe more easily and relax a bit. But it hasn't worked that way. All the end of the Cold War has meant is that we're no longer afraid of dying in a conventional – that is, nuclear – way. We're less superstitious. We think we know it all, given the Information Age and all, and since we don't have to worry about being blown off the map, we can devote all our energies to accumulating more stuff, which, after we don't have any more room for it in our houses, we put in our cottages and cars.

True, life doesn't sound so bad for people who are not starving. There is technology, there is Information, there is leisure time, all at our disposal. But it is not as simple as that. Leisure has become serious; recreation has become solemn. Somehow we have decided we must use those hours on the lakes, in the pools, and on the playing-fields to improve ourselves, make ourselves better people, healthier, with stronger hearts and firmer thighs.

Meanwhile, millions of previously enslaved people have become unenslaved and have raced to freedom, looking for vcrs, which is what we have taught them that freedom means. Arriving in free countries after passing through now-imaginary walls, they find free people telling them to go back, that there is no vcr, that there is no room and no jobs, except in berry-picking season.

It is not a world we can be extra-proud of living in, but we still have to survive in it. That means surviving the coming economic revolution, in which almost all known jobs will disappear. Resources and farms, fish and factories will not matter. The economy of the future will be based on information and parking, with a few people employed as software analysts, movie critics, and aerobics instructors. It is not a pleasant prospect, although it has its bright spots. For example, the movies will survive, in order to provide the raw material for the movie-critic industry. More on that later.

The future will also include space travel, but it will be boring and unpopular and no one will want to use it. It will be kept going mainly because we feel we owe so much to the great space pioneers, such as Buck Rogers, Mr. Spock, and Tom Corbett, Space Cadet. What that means is that escaping this world and going to another one is not a viable option. We are stuck here and have to make the best of it.

Faced with this confusion, this technological explosion, this modern multiplication of moral muddles and alliteration, how can we do right, or at least do okay? This book is for people who have often wondered about that and have wandered into the wrong aisle in the bookstore.

Chapter 2

At Work: Fighting workaholism, one workday at a time

The modern workplace expands to contain the work allotted. The work expands. It could be any place now, including some of your closets and maybe the pantry, if you have one. Many people still go to the office, but many don't. They work at home, with computers linked to the office. Or they don't work at all – a growing, mostly involuntary, trend. Many of the people who do go to the office don't confine their work to the office. They have portable, so-called laptop computers, which they carry here and there in little cases that they open up ostentatiously on airplanes. They have portable phones, which they drag out of some personal crevice in order to do business, or seem to do business, while walking down the street.

It is a paradox of the modern age: With all the business that *seems* to be getting done, with all the people talking on phones and hammering on computers in public places, businesses and government and universities don't seem to be getting any more production out of their workers than they did when workers used typewriters and telephones that dialled and were attached to the wall. So it is necessary to conclude, with no small degree of sadness, that a lot of people are just *seeming* to do business.

To be fair, they may even think they're doing business – they are talking to clients on the phone and they are accessing business-related files in their computers. It's just that none of it amounts to anything. They are really just using the telephone and using the computer because they carry the computer and the telephone around with them and they would feel guilty not hauling them out from time to time.

What does all this mean to you, an innocent, wanting only to survive, to carry on usefully without getting an ulcer and without getting knocked over in airports by racing executives swinging the latest in personal technology? It is worth noting at this juncture that the number of places in which one can find shelter from such individuals is shrinking. There has just been an announcement, published in daily newspapers, that an underwater word processor has been invented, one that is meant to aid underwater research, but that could just as easily be used for looking busy at the beach.

The first thing is not to panic. The tip-off about laptop computers is that most executives can't type. Being unable to type has traditionally gone with being an executive. The higher up the executives, the greater the probability that they can't type. This comes from an age-old assumption about typing: that it was for secretaries. Executives had important thoughts and secretaries typed them up. Generations of rising young executives noted that their bosses could not type and resolved never to learn how to type either. That was fine, even when the first computers arrived at the office: they were for secretaries to type faster on. As computers began moving into executive offices and onto the actual desks of executives, that was fine too: they gave the office a nice high-tech look and it was possible, with just a bit of training, to arrange it so that the computer was turned on and there was always something on the screen, in case a visitor should happen by.

But with laptops, all that changed – the executive had to carry the thing out into the real world and appear to be doing work on it, all this without the benefit of any typing ability at all. What to do? The answer was to have files already in the computer, after making sure the executive knew what a file was. The files would be letters, memos, documents of various sorts. Then all the busy executive had to do was learn how to *access* those files, as calling them up on the computer screen is called. Punching a few letters would, the busy executives learned, fill the screen with important amber letters and numbers, and the busy executive, seated in a crowded airplane, cocktail lounge, or exercise-club locker room, could "work" – or at least appear to.

How To Laptop

You, although you may not have thought of yourself as busy executive material, may find yourself in a position where you not only have to carry one of these things, but also have to take it out of its case and do something with it. As in so many aspects of life, the key is preparation.

1. Make sure there are files in the computer.

2. Make sure those files will not be easily understood by anyone looking over your shoulder. Numbers and abbreviations come in handy. Initials that sound like the abbreviations of airports are quite impressive.

3. The files should not have any importance or meaning.

4. Make sure you know how to access a file. All is lost if you have to ask your seatmate on the plane how to get the thing started.

Files should have names such as PRV or FLOW or – if you want to appear tough-minded – CHOP. When turned on, the computer can show all these names in a list, so it is good to make the list an impressive one. The list will be even more impressive, more computerish, if each file name is given a suffix. DOC is a common one, meaning document, but anything will do and someone can arrange it for you back at the office. A list full of things like

CHOP.DOC	PRV.TXT
FLOW.PRM	RUSH.MSG

will do the job.

With the menu, as that is called, in front of you, check to make sure your seatmate is looking and then call up one of the files. The file need not make a lot of sense. In fact, it is better if it doesn't. A collection of meaningless words and figures on a screen sends a clear message to those others who look at it that you are working on something so important that mere mortals cannot understand it.

"*124.56.*ADG," it might say. "*Rqmt uptargeted per* RGB *note re Brazil parameters. Offload prjcted at* LAX *under* NAFTA *precondits pnding* JFK OK *at source. Rqst app soonest to proceed without ref prv docs.*"

While you read the document, you should type a bit, so as to make a noise and sound as if you are working. But typing will spoil the document and make it necessary for a secretary to delete what you have typed. However, certain keys – the ALT key and the CTRL key – do nothing at all if you just hit them by themselves. So do that for a while. After that, casually type the letters "OK," followed by your initials. There. You have worked. With a bit of practice, advanced executives will learn how to take the document off the screen and put on another one, which can also, after due consideration, be okayed as well.

Advanced students, those who show real computer aptitude, can learn to vary their method of initialling the documents on the screen, substituting for the bare "OK" other, more personal phrases, such as "NOTED" and "NO OBJECTION." The ever-popular "SEE ME" carries even more weight. In adding such individual touches, there is a risk that those who can actually type might betray that fact, thus revealing themselves as not true executive material. Such embarrassment can be avoided if you keep one hand in your lap or, since the laptop is occupying the lap, by your side. Use one hand only, then, is a useful rule of thumb.

How To Counter-Laptop

There are certain advantages to being seated beside a lap-topper on an airplane. The laptopper will be so eager to show off his toys and demonstrate his importance that he is unlikely to engage in foolish chatter. Since he presumably knows little about the machine on his lap, he is unlikely to bore you with a recitation of facts about it. And since he has to "work" on his "files," he will need an atmosphere of quiet concentration. This means that you can mind your own business as he minds his.

However, it is permissible to take counter-measures if he chooses to be more aggressive in his laptopping. Certain executives like to mutter certain power phrases as they "type," phrases such as, "BG won't like this" and "That's what I call priorizing." That can be annoying and call for drastic measures, such as the following:

1. Ignoring the screen completely, you fall asleep, with your head on the laptopper's shoulder.

2. You pull a hand-held video game from your briefcase and play it enthusiastically, crying out such things as "Take that, you Gorgon beast."

3. You engage the laptopper in intense computer conversation.

This last has the most intriguing possibilities. Also it has the advantage of not making you look like a complete idiot. The key is to ask the right questions. The laptopper probably knows little about his machine. He knows how to turn it on and type his initials. The machine at hand is probably foreign to him, since he would always trade up for the latest thing as soon as he became even slightly familiar with its predecessor. In all likelihood, he knows what the salesman told him: how small it is and how powerful it is. Those are the major selling points of laptops.

Your conversation goes like this:

You: "I'm thinking about getting one of those, how do you like it?"

He: "First rate. It's got 40 megabytes and fits into my shaving-kit."

You: "How's the communications software?"

He: "Uh, fine."

You: "Do you find it slows down at all in half-duplex mode?"

He: "Not . . . um, as such."

You: "How about split-screen capability?"

He: "How . . . about those Blue Jays?"

How to Make Love to a Laptopper

Normally, one would not get involved with a person, male or female, who carries a computer. The competition for attention is too intense. There is no percentage in it. But sometimes a laptop enters a relationship after it has begun. The relationship is immediately threatened. For one thing, the laptop may occupy a lap that had previously been a place to sit. For another, an urge to impress often accompanies the computer. It will come out of its case at moments better suited to other activities.

In rare cases the presence of a laptop is a sign that its bearer actually wants to work in what you thought of as private time. At best, this is inconvenient. At worst, it signifies an unwelcome shift in priorities. Still, certain things can be done:

1. Sit on the laptop.

2. Cause embarrassing files to appear in the laptop directory, with names such as POOPSIE.DOC.

3. Fill the case with objects that signify affection, such as

flowers, chocolates, or condoms. If the computer has a pop-up screen, the effect can be dramatic.

4. Bring your own laptop to assignations. Over candlelight dinners, ask about fonts. Later, murmur about networking.

We have seen the down side of the laptop phenomenon, but there are positive aspects as well, the most prominent of which is that millions of executives around the world are made to feel and seem busy. As everybody knows, a happy executive is a productive executive. Or at least he doesn't bitch and whine quite as much.

Because laptops cause a great increase in the amount of paper generated, they help to stimulate employment. That paper has to be printed, copied, distributed, faxed, discussed, tasked, put on the agenda. All of this takes time and causes executives to work late. Never mind that all the work is caused by somebody on an airplane laboriously typing his initials; it still has to be done.

All that is good, because people need to feel busy. The modern organizational ethic (a copy of which has been surreptitiously obtained) says that nobody works less than ten hours a day. Since there is not all that much real work to be done – and most of that is being done by people and robots several layers below the executive level – there is a need to fill in time. The computer does that, and so does the phone.

On the Phone

The telephone allows busy executives to keep in touch. Keeping in touch uses up minutes, minutes become hours, and before you know it, your ten hours are up and you can go home. Keeping in touch doesn't feel like work, actually, but it looks like work, which is important, and now, with the portable cellular phone, the look of work can be taken outdoors – to your car, to your favourite sidewalk café, or just to the sidewalk.

In any city, on any street, in any airport or restaurant, even any ballpark, you can see people happily seeming to work, their voices raised just enough to let everyone know this is work, not just calling home to Mother. Even public washrooms are not immune. Listen carefully to that person you thought was just talking to himself in the third cubicle . . .

"Bobby? Chet . . . Great. Just called to keep in touch and let you know where I am . . . I'm – well, close by. Hang on a second, will you? . . . There, that's better. . . . So, what's happening?"

There is an art to cellular conversation that not all have mastered. Whatever else it accomplishes, the cellular call must communicate two facts: (1) that the caller is very busy; and (2) that he is using a cellular phone.

How To Cellular

The fact that you are using a cellular phone means that you are so busy that you must use those moments when you are in the car, the ballpark, or the movie theatre to keep in touch. And you are so important that the world must be able to keep in touch with you at all hours. If people don't realize that when they talk to you, what's the point? Here are some suggestions:

1. Always say where you are: "Hi, I'm just on my way across town, but I wanted to let you know that things are progressing." Coupled with the proper background noises (see #3 below), this should do the job, and the wording has a certain vague authority, in case you should want it to be overheard. However, in close personal relationships, the phrase "things are progressing" is not considered sufficiently warm.

2. Establish that you are busy, and underline the point that you are not just talking on an ordinary phone: "Hi, I'm just catching a quick bite in a taxi between meetings, but I wanted you to know that I'll give you a quick call later from the car."

3. Avoid quiet places. Robbed of the noise of traffic, clinking glasses, or cheering baseball fans, the phone call might as well have been made from your desk or your home, which is silly. Further, having to shout over that noise ensures that you will be heard by those around you.

4. Emphasize your lack of time by ending the conversation abruptly: "Damn! There's my stop. Gotta go. Bye." Or, more simply and more broadly: "Oops! Gotta go."

The Art of the Pseudo-Cellular

Some elements of society have already figured out that it is not necessary to buy cellular to appear cellular. In California, toy cellular phones have appeared that allow their owners to look busy in cars and other public places. That is a step forward, for if nobody really needs to keep in touch, only to *appear* to keep in touch, the disappearance of real phones in favour of toy ones would simplify our world considerably and allow long, uninterrupted baths.

In the meantime, it is worth noting that there are other ways of faking cellular status:

1. When using an ordinary telephone, play a tape of appropriate background noise and talk loudly over it. In order not to arouse suspicions, avoid certain types of background, such as roaring wild animals.

2. If no background tape is available, ask several times if you can be heard clearly.

3. If using a toy phone, avoid the kind that you pull behind you on wheels.

Some people object to hearing phones ring at the ballet or in church. They don't like overhearing other people's telephone conversations in bird sanctuaries and funeral parlours. The objection, as any busy executive can tell you, is largely on aesthetic grounds, and therefore not of substance and unlikely to be followed up by legislation. However, there are anti-cellular rumblings that are difficult to ignore.

In Japan, where a million portable phones are estimated to be on the streets, 70 per cent of them the hand-held variety, steps are being taken to make phone users conform to traditional forms of etiquette. A notice on bullet trains tells passengers that "use of portable telephones at your seat may be a disturbance to other passengers." Restaurants in the Imperial Hotel ask diners to leave their tables if the urge to keep in touch comes over them. A hotel manager is quoted by the Associated Press as saying that in the early days customers were anxious to demonstrate that they possessed a cordless phone. "But now," he said, "customers have come to understand manners."

Because our society lags far behind Japan's in the area of manners, as in many others, it is difficult to foresee in North America a sudden outbreak of sensitivity by cellular-phone users. It is also unlikely that the authorities here, always reluctant to inconvenience those who are doing business, will take any steps to restrict the busy executive's use of his or her phone. Along with that natural reluctance there is a recognition that repressive measures might be counter-productive – that they might drive the cellular phoner underground, into parking garages and subway stations.

For these reasons, cellular will win the fight to keep its visibility – visibility being one of its main reasons to exist. Every cellular owner knows: There is no point in phoning unless someone can *see* you phoning.

How To Counter-Cellular

The horrible facts outlined above show the desperate need for a counter-cellular strategy. People with telephones are invading your space. They are running into the back of your car and disrupting your baby's baptism. Fortunately, a powerful counter-strategy exists:

1. As soon as you know your caller is on a cellular, hang up. This has a certain and rather heart-warming shock value . . .

"Hello?"

"Hi, I'm just on my way to –"

"*Click.*"

(A note: Workers in certain occupations, such as those that are carried on out of a truck, have a genuine need for cellular phones. Among those are plumbers and electricians. Because it is neither polite nor wise to offend plumbers and electricians, you should ascertain first, upon being in receipt of a cellular call, the nature of the caller's business:

("Hello?"

"Hi, I'm just on my way to –"

"Are you a plumber?"

"No, I –"

"*Click.*")

2. Use the one simple phrase that brings the greatest discomfort to the cellular phoner:

"I can't hear you."

It is the perfect riposte, one to which there is no response. Picture the following conversation:

"Hello?"

"Hi, I'm just catching a quick bite on the subway between meetings, but I wanted you to know that I'll give you a quick call later from the car."

"I can't hear you."

"Just a sec. I'll move a bit. Sometimes the reception–"

"I can't hear you."

". . . RECEPTION ISN'T SO GOOD WITH THESE CELLULAR PHONES FROM THE SUBWAY. I'LL JUST TURN OFF MY LAPTOP AND MOVE IT OUT OF THE WAY. IS THAT BETTER?"

"Hello? Hello?"

The beauty of that strategy is that you can hear everything that is going on at the other end, especially the anguish of the proud owner of failed technology. And you can picture the expressions on the faces of the people around the busy executive as they watch him or her struggling to recoup.

3. Pretend to be on a cellular yourself, a slightly defective one. This enables you to garble some words, take syllables off others, whistle, growl, and make other odd noises. Drum on the mouthpiece with an HB pencil. You can also, as shown previously, play your own background tape, including wild animal sounds.

"...O?"

"Hi, I'm just on the 401, passing the Yonge exit, and I had a minute on the way to –"

"BELCH WHISTLE –upid HONK FLEEP FLEEP –ucker. OOGA-OOGA."

"Can you hear me all right?"

"–ine. SSSSSSS GURGLE MOO. –ssed off. ROARRR! GONG. –amn bozo phoning ZINGZINGZING."

"Hello?"

That strategy, enjoyable as it may be for the sophisticated and well-equipped person, has the disadvantage of requiring much preparation and a considerable investment in time and equipment. For the great majority of people, the best strategy is a simple: "I can't hear you!" used strategically at various points in the conversation. For example, it is fun to let the caller run through his entire speech about where he is and how busy he is before the first "I can't hear you." But it is good also to interrupt the sentences that seem to mean the most to the caller. You have to use your own good judgment.

4. Often in a restaurant or other public place a person nearby will size up the situation, check the crowd, and decide to put on a telephone show for your benefit. There are several tactics worth trying here. One is to hand the caller a little printed card: "HELLO," the card will say. "I AM NOT A DEAF PERSON AND CAN HEAR EVERY WORD YOU SAY. PLEASE GIVE ME $25 SO I CAN TAKE A TAXI SOMEWHERE ELSE."

5. A more common tactic is disruption. This consists of waiting until the busy executive has connected and then making enough noise to be overheard at the other end – or at least to make the phoner fear that you will be overheard at the other end. What you say is up to you. College fight songs have been shown to be effective. For men, thumping on the table accompanied by shouts of "Take it off, honey!" can also work. Women can loudly inquire, "Shall I get you another drink before we get started?" Perhaps the dart that goes closest to the heart is a direct attack on the phoner's identity. This is done by raising the voice and saying:

"Listen to this, everybody. He's pretending he's talking on a cellular phone!"

6. Sometimes none of this is practical. There may be a rule against fight songs, or the phoner may be large and mean-looking. At that point the fall-back position is simply to go with the flow. This means implicitly acknowledging the busy executive's right to have his phone, and asking to use it.

There is a knack to doing this. Busy executives are happy to show off their phones, most of which cost hundreds of dollars and have many impressive features, but there is also a reluctance to share something that is so intensely personal.

Flattery is the way around that, a strong play to the busy executive's pride in his possession.

"Excuse me, but I couldn't help noticing that phone. Is it yours?"

"Yes. I couldn't live without it."

"It looks like it's got quite a few impressive features."

"That's right. It has a 150-number alpha-numeric memory, has a built-in alarm clock, plus an anti-theft device and a messaging system."

"Gee, mine hasn't got half that stuff. Would you mind if I tried it out?"

Then, punching out the number you have memorized for

just this purpose, you telephone a friend who is on the bullet train for Tokyo.

Meanwhile Back at the Shop

Given all these technological improvements, there are not too many people at the office these days, aside from those who are actually doing the work. Their main concern is quite different from those out in the field with their phones and laptop computers. It is to keep at a distance the pieces of paper generated by the executives with the laptop computers and the phone messages generated by the people with the portable phones. Above all, it is to fend off the managerial impulses of those busy executives who somehow remain at the office.

Such people have absorbed the *Creed of the Busy Executive*, which is to:

1. Walk fast and carry a piece of paper.
2. Never smile at someone less important than you.
3. Never stop to small-talk with anyone who can't advance your career.

The question facing you who are not busy executives is: How to deal with such people so that you can get your work done and still get home in time for dinner? There are some new ideas, as well as some time-honoured strategies that will be familiar to you. It is worth noting that times have changed, and time has passed by some of the time-honoured strategies, so that they are no longer honoured.

How to Survive in the Workplace

1. *Be a complete dodo.* This used to work. Wearing badly fitting, out-of-date clothes, pretending that you couldn't type, work a calculator, or find the elevator used to qualify you as a genius. The company would keep you around because it was feared that you knew something. This is not a clever strategy now, in the computer age. There is too much paper to be

moved and no time to look for elevators, according to the latest management studies. Reading management studies about the shortage of time now takes up a considerable portion of each workday.

2. *Master the technology.* This is not an inviting prospect for the non-energetic. Learning a new computer program, for example, is hard work. Worse, once you master it, you will be expected to work it. The up side is that you will be the only one who knows how to work it. Busy executives, as we have learned, have an aversion to typing that spreads to the actual use of computers. If you learn the program, you will have a monopoly of expertise. It means that when you leave the office, the work stops, and it cannot start until you return. There is potential power there, should you want to use it. Of course, you don't want to use it, because if you did you would be promoted and have to walk fast, carry a piece of paper, and stop small-talking with your former friends. But even if you don't use it, the fact that you could use it, should you choose to do so, can be put to good use, particularly in forcing busy executives to keep their distance.

3. *Be dangerous.* This follows from #2 above. If your superiors do not quite understand you, if they think you are a little – how to put this delicately? – nuts, if they are a bit afraid of what you will do if pushed too far, you are in pretty good shape. The modern corporation (which definition also includes the modern university, the modern hospital, and the modern government) prides itself on being able to tolerate diversity, even if it doesn't really like diversity all that much. So if you dress down, smoke, growl, and make a point of suddenly leaving meetings for no reason at all, there is a good chance that you will survive, perhaps even advance. At the point when the modern corporation is tempted to fire you, the thought nags at the back of the modern corporation's mind that it is only firing you because it doesn't like you. The modern corporation hates to think of itself as being that sort

of guy. So you will be kept on as long as you like, assuming that you can find the elevators.

4. *Be counter-busy.* There is a corporate ethic, as we all know. It is continually shifting, but the successful busy executive is able to keep up, to remember whether he is supposed to kick butt or be supportive this year. This is hard work, and sometimes there is a bit of envy of the worker who seems indifferent to it all, who doesn't seem to need the work at all. Cultivating that image can cause your superiors to value you more. When they sense that you don't need the job, they will spend time and energy, perhaps even money, trying to convince you that the job needs you. You cultivate the image by working part-time, by leaving early, by phoning in reports from the cottage, by taking leaves of absence to pursue your freelance canoe-building career. If you are successful, you will be wooed beyond your wildest dreams. And even if you are not, the strategy won't tax your energy levels.

The modern office has pressures that never occurred to the pioneers. When a water-cooler was invented that could make a great big bubble rise to the surface after a paper cup of water was poured, the pioneers thought nothing would be able to top that. As we have seen, technology has gone well past that, bringing new pressures. In addition, theories of management have progressed. Today there is an entire economy based upon meetings, upon importing psychologists and animators to help busy executives become more synergistic. There are expensive retreats at which busy executives talk about cutting costs. There are seminars about computer security and improved lunching techniques. All of this raises questions, which, in turn, raise answers, which is as it should be.

Q. What is the significance of the rise of balloonograms in the modern office, and is there anything I should be doing about it?

A. The balloonogram sector is one of the few areas of consistent growth in the modern economy. People are always celebrating birthdays and whatnot in the modern workplace, and what could be more natural than for someone dressed as a clown to waddle into the office carrying balloons and singing a song?

Your question indicates that you think there is something that should be "done" about balloonograms. This is wrongheaded. Even if you are not fond of clowns (in official costume) appearing in your workplace, it is well to avoid offending such people. Balloonogram work provides employment for many people who are temporarily between engagements. One of them may, upon regaining previous heights, be your employer, or potential employer. So you should resist the temptation to say such things as "Why don't you go back where you came from, you stupid clown!" for several reasons:

1. The clown may some day be a busy executive. A tip-off is if he is waddling fast and carrying a piece of paper.

2. Clowns are the only people who can pass through building security without having to produce identification. So the clown you insult may be a terrorist who will carry you away and cause you to miss lunch.

3. Clowns don't like to be called clowns. They like to be called "people living with red noses and oversized feet."

Q. My boss has begun telling me I look tired. Yesterday when he walked past my desk he even slowed down as he talked to me. What does this mean?

A. If you are female and your boss is male, it means that he is about to follow up his observation with an improper suggestion. So say right away, "I know. I'm going home right now to rest," and then leave. In all other circumstances, it means that your boss has taken a course on how to relate to the modern worker. He (or she) has learned the importance of empathy and is trying to demonstrate a caring nature. Saying you look tired is about the only thing that comes to mind. (Similarly, if the boss says, "How about those Expos?" in the middle of hockey season, you will know another course is under way.) And you will know that the course has really had an impact if the boss actually comes to a complete stop at your desk.

Q. Some of my older colleagues often talk in nostalgic terms about "the old office lunch." What was this, and should I be trying to bring it back?
A. The old office lunch to which your colleagues refer lasted longer than the twenty-three minutes it does today. People drank alcohol and smoked cigarettes. They did not put their telephones on the table. In most cases, they didn't carry telephones at all. The lunch was out of the building, not at the desks of workers. Workers did not bring reports to read at the table. Diet was also different from what it is today. People ate steaks and hamburgers and sandwiches containing eggs and cheese and meat, and other food substances high in cholesterol and fat. Salads were not available in most restaurants, except as side dishes consisting mainly of lettuce. Smoking took place right at the table, rather than in a doorway to the outside.

These lunches sometimes lasted more than two hours. There was unnecessary laughter at them. When our society decided that there was no time for that, and that work and diet should be taken more seriously, it was inevitable that the office lunch would undergo reconsideration. Among certain types of people there is a fondness for the old office lunch, but it was clearly unproductive and contributed to a decline in efficiency. As for the supposed benefits to company morale of the office lunch, these can be adequately replaced by sensitivity seminars for both employees and management.

Q. Every day there are love letters in my computer. They are very affectionate and nice but I am disturbed that

someone seems to have my secret personal computer access number. How do I find out who is writing the letters and is such a person the type with whom I should have a relationship?

A. To answer your last question first, probably not. You would probably be entering into a relationship with a person who works in the computer department, with all that this entails. You can test that by looking closely at the letters. Does the person use words such as "transfer" when dealing with intimate subjects? Does the person address you by number rather than by name? If so, it is someone who knows computers too well.

The Rise and Fall of
Men and Women and Vice Versa

By the time you read this, all that difficult business of promoting women because they are women, or *appearing* to promote women because they are women, even if that is not the reason, or, on the other hand, backlashing by promoting men because they are men – all that may be over. On the other hand, it may not. An entire industry has arisen concerned with deciding who is fair and who is unfair and whether different groups have been discriminated against as opposed to empowered, or whether they have been empowered too much and should now be disempowered. Thousands of people have found employment dealing with such questions, researching them, sitting on boards, taking each other to court and so on. Massive unemployment would result if it was suddenly decided that the workplace was operating fairly. And since the workplace rarely operates fairly anyway, there is little chance of that happening.

Our society has become increasingly sophisticated at discovering new forms of unfairness, and there is no reason to think that will stop. By the new century, new criteria may be found – the old sexual, racial, linguistic, and disabled criteria not being enough. There may be real or perceived discrimination in favour of, or against, people who sit in certain types of chairs, or sit in them in a certain way. Slouchers may seek empowerment. People who sit up straight may worry about not getting enough of the good jobs. Height may finally become the factor many had feared, or hoped, it would be. Who can tell? We can only proceed on the basis of what we know.

In the meantime, certain traditional rituals in the workplace have become fraught with danger. New contexts require a new etiquette.

Congratulations on a Promotion

No one knows any more whether Person A got the job because of or in spite of his or her sex, race, or language, or because his or her main competition, Person B, was of a different sex, race, or language, or whether Person A just got the job because Person A was the best person – putting aside for the moment the theory that the concept of "best" is rooted in a traditional and stereotyped way of looking at things – or whether management just flipped a coin.

Despite all these doubts and fears, certain traditions still remain, such as taking Person A out for a congratulatory drink after work. At that celebration, there are a few things it is permissible to say. Among them:

1. "I'm sure you got it on the basis of your abilities."
2. "Looks like rain."

If Person B is along, as he or she might be, not wanting to appear a bad sport, it is appropriate to say to him or her:

1. "Looks like rain."
2. "Don't worry. It's a sloucher's turn next time."

Congratulations on Retirement

In less complicated times, you always knew what to say when someone retired. "Congratulations," you'd say, and then:

"I can't believe you're 65." Now it is different. You have no way of knowing if the retiree is 65. Retirement begins at 55, with a buy-out, or even earlier if the organization wants to get rid of the person really badly. It does not fall within the realm of flattery to tell a 49-year-old that you can't believe he's 65. On the other hand, you don't want to suggest to someone who has toiled all the way to 65 that she's been bought out. And there's always the chance that the person retiring should have retired years ago. And saying that it looks like rain has been done to death. So what *do* you say?

1. "The place won't be the same without you." No one can be offended by that one, even if what you mean is that the place will be much better.

2. "I bet you could write a book about this place." This doesn't mean you will read it. On the other hand, it might plant an interesting idea in the mind of a disgruntled 49 year old.

3. "I hear it's going to be warmer."

How To Feign Plain Speaking While Still Obfuscating

So much time has been wasted, so much money lost, because people have learned how to avoid saying what they mean. The avoidance of meaning sprang from understandable impulses: People worried that others might be offended if they understood what was said; they worried that saying something understandable might lead to criticism and that they might be held accountable for their words if others knew what they meant. Such fears produced current modes of writing and speaking in business and government. People have prospered by mastering the art of speaking and writing without meaning, but the practice has attracted a considerable amount of ridicule and a reaction has set in, called plain speaking.

Because it challenges the accumulated momentum of

decades of bureaucracy, plain speaking will probably never catch on, but it will be necessary, at least for a time, to appear to master it. At the moment, managers like to think of themselves as no-nonsense communicators, and they want to think of you the same way. They have taken courses in plain speaking, given by the latest generation of snake-oil salesmen, and they will send you on similar courses if they value you enough.

Although the dangers of plain speaking are well known, you must still speak plainly. Or seem to. Here, it is essential to remember that certain key phrases give the appearance of bluntness and directness. Using them, you can engage in plain speaking without disrupting meetings or destroying the special relaxed qualities that a good memo possesses:

1. "I'm sorry that I have to be blunt about this, but I think your position has certain attributes that merit further consideration."

2. "If we pursue our present course, there are almost certain to be consequences, one way or another. I could not forgive myself if I didn't say that."

3. "Let's stop beating around the bush. In a nutshell, it comes down to this: We can't have it both ways and we're kidding ourselves if we think we can. That's the way I feel, and if someone doesn't like it, so be it."

If you say something like this at a meeting, thump the table.

A Note on Voice Mail

Management, in its wisdom and in order to lay off several switchboard operators, has purchased a voice-mail system. This means that a caller, instead of hearing an operator say that you are not there, will hear a recording of your voice saying that you are not there. Courses have been offered, which you skipped, teaching you how to get the most out of this innovation. Plain speaking dictates that you should let callers know exactly where you are and when you will be back. Reality dictates that if you wanted to talk on the phone you would have stayed at your desk, and the last thing you want is a bunch of messages telling you to phone people. Technology dictates that management may be monitoring the messages you leave on your machine. Your dilemma can be solved by applying some of the principles of pseudo-plain speaking to your voice mail:

"Hello, I'm away from my desk but will be back. In the meantime, I want you to know that I value your call. Thank you."

Notice how pleasant and considerate the message is. Notice also that it doesn't say where you are or when you will be back. Notice, finally, that it doesn't ask the caller to leave a message.

At work, we make hard choices every day. We must do the right thing at the same time as we seem to do the accepted thing. If we do the accepted thing too often – such as carrying the phone out onto the golf course, or spending too many lunch hours at salad bars – we risk losing the ability to recognize what the right thing is. At the same time, if doing the right thing consistently causes consistent unemployment, how moral is that, eh?

The key, as we have seen, is to play the game and float above it at the same time. This would seem to require unusually long arms, but it can be done, as long as you get plenty of recreation and frequent naps.

Chapter 3

At Play: Honouring the tortoise

How To Be Fit, or at Least Fitting

How To Stay Married to a Fitness Fanatic

How To Make Love to a Fitness Fanatic

Effortless Superiority Is the Best Kind

Riding a Bicycle Without Being a Geek

Winning at Non-Competitive Games

Even Stranger Recreational Forms

How To Dome

How To Be a Cottage Guest

The Rules for Cottage Hosts

Leisure used to be leisurely. Now it is not. Now all leisure is competitive and all competition is an industry. Leisure is a misnomer.

For proof, all you need to know is this: At a major bass-fishing tournament in Northern Ontario, lie-detector tests have been put in place for the winners. It was decided to do this when fish pens were discovered in the lake, leading to the suspicion that larger fish were being brought in from other lakes, kept in the pens, and then produced as if freshly caught for the purpose of winning the huge cash prizes available, as well as the corporate sponsorships by outboard-motor and rod-and-reel companies that could go with the cash prizes.

You remember fishing. You put on your old clothes and your lucky hat, got into the boat, and set out quietly in the early evening, hoping to catch something but reasonably content just to catch a good sunset. You trolled slowly around the lake or maybe sat quietly at a spot that might have fish in it or might not, but was pretty anyway. Meanwhile, you listened to your pulse rate slow down.

There was lying, sure, when you got back to the cottage.

The one that you almost landed was at least this big, maybe bigger, certainly much larger than anything anyone had caught, or not caught, for years. But the lying was not for cash prizes, only for the entertainment of the group, and anyway you almost believed it yourself. Now they are out there in these state-of-the-art fishing boats, incredibly fast boats equipped with radar and sonar and digital computer read-outs of this and that, the fishermen sitting in swivel chairs so as not to tire, wearing the logos of corporate sponsors on every inch of their clothing. Off they go, 900 miles an hour across the lake to the spot indicated by the sonar or the radar, where rapid-fire fishing takes place for approximately seven minutes, then 900 miles an hour across to the other side of the lake, fish fish fish, then 900 miles an hour somewhere else. So as not to waste a minute.

Leisure has come to this. You remember bicycles. You climbed onto your two-wheeler and pedalled slowly up the hills, coasted down. If you had any gears that worked, you shifted when you remembered to do so. If somebody came bicycling by in the other direction, you waved and smiled. Now people put on skin-tight spandex outfits, clip a plastic water bottle filled with some nutrient-enhanced liquid onto the bicycle, choose one of thirty-six gears, and set out, monitoring their heartbeat, their kilometres per hour, the wind speed, and their blood pressure. They go as fast as they can, checking frequently in the rear-view mirror attached to their helmets to make sure nobody behind is going faster. To the extent that it is possible to do so without slowing down, they avoid pedestrians, dogs, and slower bicycles, but they never wave, never smile.

Leisure has come to this. The Japanese invented karaoke, an innocent pastime in which drunken businessmen in bars got to hold onto a microphone and pretend they were Frank Sinatra or perhaps Kyu Sakamoto. A machine would play background music and they would belt it out – "Night and

Day" or "McArthur Park"– to the applause of their drinking companions. Now karaoke has come to North America. There are karaoke bars along Highway 17, north of Parry Sound, which means there is one near you, wherever you are. And there are are competitions, tournaments in suburban roadhouses and small-town bars, the winners taking home big prizes and qualifying for the semi-finals and the national finals, which could lead to overbooked hotels if they happen to coincide with the national finals in aerobics, video games, trivia, or bird-watching.

Their existence has not been proven, but it is easy to suspect that there are professional karaoke hustlers, moving from roadhouse to roadhouse across this continent, luring the suckers with mediocre renditions of "Let It Be" and then cashing in big, double or nothing, with flawlessly crafted, dramatically paced versions of "New York, New York" and "Blowin' in the Wind."

Similarly, you know that every cottagers' association has a triathlon in which its members run, cycle, and paddle, and that such events are invaded by triathlon hustlers from the big city. And you know, in your heart, that there are trivia hustlers out there, maybe even birding sharpies, travelling the circuit to scoop the prizes and land the lucrative birding shoe endorsements.

Leisure has become hard work. We used to do a little of this and a little of that to keep fit – or at least a little bit fit. If not fit, not fat, anyway. Now we can compete to see how fit we are, maybe even reaching the fitness finals. In the privacy of our homes, waiting for the late movie, we see entire hours devoted to commercials for gleaming structures that will put muscles where they should be, eliminate unsightly lumps, and make our hearts fairly purr with health.

Before the modern age, we jumped a little and stretched a bit and ran and whatnot, and if there was pain we stopped and if the pain stayed on for a couple of days we went to the doctor, after which we spent a pleasurable week or so lying down. We used to jog in the park for fifteen minutes or until the dog got tired. Now we are warned that serious harm could result unless we do twenty minutes of stretching exercises before our fifteen-minute run. And, of course, the dog has to do his exercises too.

We can never be too careful. Nowadays, we avoid the risk of injury *before gardening* through a series of carefully structured warm-up exercises. Gardening, we are warned in the media, is more than just scratching around pleasantly in the dirt and cutting worms in half to stage races. Injury, such as Pruner's Thumb, can result unless we carefully prepare ourselves. Leisure has become solemn.

Look at the grim faces of the parents as they watch their kids at T-ball or soccer – fearful that they might get hurt, fearful that they might be too competitive, fearful that they might lose. The grim-faced kids are worried that they might not be good enough, or might be too good, or might not enjoy themselves enough, or might do something that the book says they shouldn't. Listen, in vain, for the laughter around the softball diamonds, basketball courts, hockey arenas, and touch-football fields, where grown men and women relax, supposedly, in their leisure hours. Listen to the grunts on the neighbourhood tennis courts. Try to find a smile on the golf course. It is a serious business.

And certainly a business. Every activity has its appropriate outfit, its requisite gear. There are shoes for baseball, football, racquet sports, volleyball, running, aerobics, walking, hiking, and, if you are not quite sure, shoes for something called cross-training. There are hats for bicycling, shirts for aerobics, jackets for birding. There are clothes for spectating, perhaps the biggest sellers of all – each with the logo of a professional or a university team. The logo business itself is big, with team logos attaching to pens, cups, dishes, lighters, pennants, seat cushions, thermoses, and all manner of unrelated clothing, such as a cowboy hat in brown corduroy decorated with the Montreal Expos logo. You undoubtedly have your personal favourite. Perhaps it is a toothbrush.

Where it will lead is difficult to say. Perhaps it will be the karaoke outfit, most likely a spandex version of the drunken Japanese businessman look.

Can we possibly relax in such an environment, a world in which there is stiff competition between the manufacturers of non-competitive games? *Should* we relax in such an environment? Can we relax but win maybe every once in a while? After all, there is nothing sacred about losing. The thing to do is set attainable goals.

How To Be Fit, or at Least Fitting

There are several choices:

1. *Buy all the clothes, do all the exercises.* This is the obvious choice, but is too costly and too time-consuming.

2. *Buy all the clothes.* This is expensive, but more restful. If looking appropriate is important to you, you can try this. The trick is to appear in your outfit as if you *have just come back from* doing the thing you are dressed up to do. If you learn a few of the right phrases, you can develop a reputation as a runner, a bicyclist, even a volleyball player.

"Boy, it was hot out there," you can say, not lying at all, as you towel off.

Water splashed on your forehead can masquerade as sweat. If volleyball is your choice, you will have to find some sand to put on. If you choose a competitive sport, someone will invariably ask if you won. Don't say you kicked butt, which is crude and boastful and may lead to one of your friends trying to match you up with someone who actually plays the game. Say: "It was a good game," and smile modestly. People will then think that you are either a graceful loser, or someone who is too good a sport to say he kicked butt.

3. Do all the exercises. This is not recommended, unless you are a total Spartan and a fitness fanatic, in which case you would not be having anything to do with a book unless it was on a cassette player attached to your home rowing-machine. Why do the exercise without getting any of the clothes? Some of the clothes are neat, excepting the bicycle shorts.

4. *Mix and match.* Play tennis in your bicycle outfit (although bicycle get-up is intrinsically silly and may cause you to attempt to shift gears on your tennis racquet). Sing karaoke in tennis whites. A good song would be "Red River Volley," but you probably have your own thoughts. The idea here is to get as much exercise as you think you need while at the same time demonstrating that you have not been caught up completely in leisure marketing.

5. *Practise the Theory of Stylistic Erstwhilability.* In other words, stay one style behind. Wearing the previous decade's outfit may mark you as square, but that is a risk you must be prepared to take, unless you want to spend your whole life in spandex and Velcro. And in fact, wearing last decade's outfit can mark you as an individualist, which is not always bad. That's how you should be thinking, as you trudge along the cross-country ski trails in your corduroy knickers. "I am not outdated; I am me." Or: "I am I," if you like your grammar to be just so.

Plus, it's cheaper. That can be a consolation to you the year when the entire world regains its senses and wears nice earth colours and you are in hot pink on a lime-green bicycle, trying to be inconspicuous.

How To Stay Married to a Fitness Fanatic

You could become a fitness fanatic yourself, but that would be wrong. The best way to stay married to a fitness fanatic is to help him, or her, overcome the addiction to fitness.

1. Defeat her at everything.
2. Tell him his muscles are too obvious – and that you hate that muscle-bound look.
3. Starch the spandex.

How To Make Love to a Fitness Fanatic

1. During sex, murmur compliments on your partner's muscle tone.
2. After sex, share a carrot.

Effortless Superiority Is the Best Kind

In the world of leisure, it used to be easy to go slow: you chose a bicycle over a car, a canoe over a motorboat, a sailboard over a water ski, cross-country skis over downhill ones. Lately there has been an alarming development. The leisure industry has adapted all the things you like to go slow with and made them go fast. Cross-country skiers can now use the skating technique to zoom along the trails. Sailboats and sailboards race through the water and leap over the waves in beer commercials. We have already seen about fishermen and bicyclists. The humble water pistol, once a symbol of innocent child's play, now holds gallons of water, and has the range of a mortar shell and the capacity to injure. The International Water Pistol Classic awaits only the signing of a corporate sponsor.

In the face of all this rushing by, what is your proper role?

1. *Go really slow.* The slower you go, the more it is clear that you are doing it on purpose, and maybe could go fast if you felt like it. You don't care what people think anyway, but there is no point in their thinking that the reason you are going slow is that you are slow.

2. *Neither sweat nor grunt.* If you are to lose anyway, it is better not to have too much psychic energy involved in the result. Grunting, swearing, and wiping your brow on your

shirt send out the wrong signals, enabling your opponent to take far too much satisfaction in victory. On the other hand, winning without grunting or sweating is particularly sweet.

3. *Honour the tortoise.* The most vital fact about the tortoise is not that it won, but that it avoided making an idiot of itself. Think about it: No child has ever been urged to emulate a hare. Even if the tortoise had lost, it would probably have been the crowd favourite. And even if it had lost, it would have been able to say to itself, and to anyone else who was listening: "Hey, after all, I'm just a tortoise." And, finally, no tortoise ever had to do twenty minutes' worth of exercises *after* the race.

Riding a Bicycle Without Being a Geek

There is no reason for you to give up your bicycle just because the roadways and bike paths have become a riot of spandex. The Tortoise Principle can be combined with the Theory of Stylistic Erstwhilability to produce many happy hours on two wheels.

1. Always be at least one gear higher than anyone else. That means your legs are pumping more slowly and it looks as if you don't care how fast you are going, although you could be going quite fast.

2. Be sure to say "Beep-beep" to other cyclists as you overtake them.

3. Be sure to say "Lovely day!" to other cyclists as they overtake you.

4. Dress as if you were going to do something else – play softball, for example – and just happened to put a helmet on.

5. In order to avoid any suggestion of excessive competitiveness, make sure your helmet is covered with stickers commemorating such things as jazz festivals and scenic caves.

6. Always choose corduroy over spandex.

Winning at Non-Competitive Games

Competition has been misunderstood by many. Out of the sixties mentality came the notion that trying to win produced monsters who caused the Vietnam War. Nowadays we know different. We know that there is nothing wrong with winning, as long as you don't become a complete jerk trying to do it. Meanwhile, however, we are occasionally faced with situations in which we are required to play co-operatively. The goal here is to enjoy the game, winning if the rules allow it, at the same time as you avoid appearing to have participated in the Bombing of Cambodia.

1. *Be the first to help the others.* Show them what to do at every turn. Skip your turn occasionally. Remind the others, particularly if they are children, that the aim is not to win. With any luck they will quickly decide to switch to badminton, or even solitaire.

2. Should you, by some accident, win a game that is supposed to be non-competitive, remind your opponents that it is a victory for all of you.

3. Should your non-competitors not take this well, suggest to them that non-competitiveness is a declining concept in today's world. So it shouldn't matter if they don't win at it.

Even Stranger Recreational Forms

There is more to leisure than playing sports. There is also watching sports. In its traditional form, spectating has been around for centuries. People gathered beside a tennis court or hockey rink and cheered on the participants. In our age, however, spectating has taken on new forms that need to be understood, in order to enjoy them more fully or avoid them altogether.

Modern sports facilities, typified by the domed stadium, are not the same as the older ones. Through the wonders of technology, the domed stadium can offer a state-of-the-art sound system, to keep spectators entertained with music between pitches, and a scoreboard with space-age technology, to offer them all the benefits of the Information Age. These include advertisements, opportunities to choose, through applause, the song that will be played after the next inning, and notification as to the proper time to call out "CHARGE!" In addition, the camera roams through the crowd and gives spectators the chance to see themselves on the scoreboard. Because of technology, coupled with such innovations as the Wave, the modern stadium has become interactive. No longer do people just sit there and watch athletes perform. Now people can become part of the show themselves.

Being a spectator has become competitive, in other words. Spectators compete by seeking to be noticed, by the scoreboard camera, and by any network TV that happens to be in the building. They take their shirts off, particularly if the temperature is below freezing. They paint their faces. They hold up signs that contain the call letters of the network broadcasting the game. They conduct dramatic demonstrations of self-congratulation if they capture a foul ball. They wave whenever they think a camera might be in the neighbourhood. And of course they do the Wave, which consists of standing up suddenly and shrieking, in conjunction with others in the same section. Everybody's a star in the Dome Age.

How To Dome

1. To make the camera notice you, wear a large animal head. If the animal represents one of the teams, you will be competing with many other such animals and may be overlooked. It is not wise, in other words, to dress up like a lion if you are at a Detroit Lions game. If you dress up like an octopus, however, you have a chance. The cameras will pick you out during a time out and one of the commentators will chuckle and say something like: "Hey, it takes all kinds."

You will be the envy of your section, and you will have six extra hands to carry beers.

2. If you choose not to be interactive, if you simply want to watch the game in peace, remember that beer can be a weapon as well as a drink. A carefully spilled cup of beer can keep away mascots and people dressed up as lions. It takes quite some time to get the beer out of a lion costume, and you will be left alone during that period.

3. If all else fails, hail an usher and demand that the lion be ejected from the stadium. This will never work, of course. Some lions are, in fact, employed by the stadium. But it will cause a commotion and inspire people to yell "Sit down!" at the lion, which is probably bigger than you. The lion will be embarrassed. If it is employed by the stadium, it will stay out of your section. If it is just a private citizen, it may take its head off for the rest of the game.

4. Remarks addressed to a child can help get your message across to would-be interactives in your section. Older children can be trained to feed the appropriate leading questions:

Child: "Mommy, when can I do the Wave?"

You: "Not today, honey. I'm afraid there's a rule against it."

In cities where people are especially law-abiding, such as Toronto, this will be sufficient. In other places, a different message must be conveyed, aimed at the spot where people are most vulnerable, their fear of being in bad taste.

Child: "Daddy, look! They're doing the Wave."

You: "Oh really? That went out in New York two years ago."

5. Don't encourage the scoreboard by reacting to anything on it. If you must do something during stoppages in play, read a book.

6. Whatever you do, make sure your children learn the Credo of the Non-Competitive Sports Fan: "It's not whether you win or lose, it's how you watch the game."

Other contemporary forms of leisure which there is no space to go into here, and not much inclination either, include yoga, square-dancing, and lurching around on whatever variation of roller skates the department stores are stocking these days. Leisure is an ever-shifting field, as they always say at soccer games during small earthquakes. Certain activities come, such as volleyball, others go, such as painting by numbers. (Although watch for a revival when painting by numbers goes digital.) In the years ahead, leisure activities will be closely related to escaping urban pressures. That's why some day soon you are going to find yourself freezing to death in a boat surrounded by mosquitoes, another unwitting victim of the summer cottage boom. With certain simple guidelines in mind, however, it is possible to emerge intact and get on with what remains of your life.

How To Be a Cottage Guest

Even a wilderness needs rules, otherwise it becomes wild. Cottage guests, new to the wilderness and susceptible to attack from many directions, need rules more than anyone else. The following, the Official Rules for Cottage Guests, have been developed over a period of centuries, although no one has written them down before. You know how busy people get.

1. Don't expect your hosts to meet you on time. If they have been at at the cottage for more than a week, their metabolism has slowed and they have lost their sense of urgency. When they ask if you have been waiting long, say no: you got lost on the way. While some cottage people pride themselves on the precision of the directions they give, most take a secret pride in staying at a place that is hard to find, particularly if they can find it themselves.

2. Do not feel it is necessary to appear in nautical gear. Many cottage people do not, themselves, wear yachtsmen's caps, and will not be offended if you do not bring one.

3. Comment only favourably upon the cottage and its surroundings. Avoid using the words "quaint" and "cute." Do not, even when trying to keep the conversation going, offer to help fix something, such as a badly fitting door, that appears to need fixing. It may have just been fixed.

4. Do not feel that you have to comment upon everything, even favourably. Saying: "Oh, what a nice lifejacket" is probably going too far. Compliments on certain aspects of nature, such as a towering white pine, will be graciously received; compliments on seagulls are overdoing it.

5. Many rules of city conversation also apply at the cottage, a fact that some guests, trying for the proper tone of informality, forget. A beer before dinner is never a "drinkie-poo." Likewise, dinner is not "grub."

6. Dinner table conversation will be about what is happening at the cottage, such as the sighting of various animals and birds. It will not be about what is happening at the office. If they are missing something, hosts do not want to know.

7. Some hosts have a rule that guests will not help with the dishes on their first day. Hosts who have that rule will be sure to let you know. Otherwise, help with the dishes. In helping with the dishes, you do not need to comment upon the absence of a dishwasher. The hosts likely know that. If the hosts do, however, have a dishwasher, it is not wise to refer to the "good old days" before cottages had labour-saving devices.

8. It is permissible, but not absolutely necessary, to have sex at the cottage, assuming that your papers are in order. If you choose to do so, remember that walls are thin, and sound carries, and that any pet nicknames or cries of encouragement you employ will live on in the folklore of the cottage. If that is not what you want, remember that muffled grunts can be passed off the next morning as having been made by something whose eyes you saw in a tree.

9. The first question asked of any guest in the morning is:

"How did you sleep?" The answer is: "Fine." That is the only appropriate answer, although "Very well" is acceptable. Your answer will elicit follow-up questions concerning whether the lumpiness of the bed bothered you. The answer is: "No."

10. Ascertain quickly whether the hosts intend you to participate in work projects. Some hosts have projects; some don't. Some have plans; some just go to the dock as soon as the breakfast dishes are done. Never ask: "What's the plan?" unless you know that your host has one. And never, never, never have a plan of your own.

11. Avoid comparisons. The fact that you have seen, at other cottages, nicer buildings, faster boats, smarter children, older canoes, bigger fish, better-functioning septic systems, dogs better suited to the wilds – none of these facts has the slightest relevance to the situation in which you find yourself.

12. Size up the prevailing ethic. Some cottages are for drinking; some are for loud fun in the sun; some are for sitting quietly and reading; some are for afternoon naps; some are for working. You can't read while your hosts work. More important, you can't work while your hosts nap. Your hosts did not invite you up to make them feel guilty.

13. Just as you have to adapt to your hosts' ways, your children have to adapt to the hosts' children's ways. That may mean walking through the woods, examining plants and admiring different forms of wildlife. But probably not. More likely, the accepted form of activity will consist of lying around inside a dark cottage on a sunny day, playing Monopoly, reading *Archie* comics, and listening to tapes of rap or thrash or techno-pop or whatever it is.

14. Be prepared to play games after dinner. Also, be prepared for dinner to be called supper. Hosts have certain rituals that are more likely to manifest themselves at the cottage than in civilian life. Among those may be bridge games, or rummy games, or games you have never heard of, played

with noise and enthusiasm, plus a shocking degree of competitiveness, right around the time you thought you would be curled up with a mystery. You might as well play, lose, and be a good sport. There are no alternatives. No host in his right mind has a television set.

Guests are not the only ones who have rules to observe, a fact hosts sometimes forget. Life is more pleasant if they don't.

The Rules for Cottage Hosts

1. You did not invent the scenery. Stop bragging about it.

2. You don't have to show guests photographs of the cottage. They are at it.

3. Let guests know what the house rules are: Do you flush at all times, or not? Do you *like* the raccoons? Which end of the canoe is the front? Don't allow guests to violate the unwritten rules and then laugh at them.

4. Don't go charging off into the woods without your guests, hammering and sawing and making loud working noises, then come back and say: "Oh, when did you get up?"

5. Don't think you can change the rules of badminton and cribbage just because it's your cottage.

6. Don't tell guests how much fun other guests were.

7. Guests are not afraid, just this once, to overeat; don't be afraid to overfeed.

8. Don't apologize for the weather. Guests know it's not your fault, and they know it's always better than this.

9. Guests don't need to know as much about the septic system as you think they do.

Chapter 4

In the City: Great place to live, bad place to park

How To Beat the Traffic

How To Amaze Your Friends with Parking Anecdotes

What If You Are Unfortunate Enough To Own a Car?

Surviving the Real Estate Conversation

How To Be Fashionable

How To Be Unfashionable and Survive

Q & A: How To Be a Great City-Dweller,
Even in a Small City

In the city, all conversational roads lead to roads and all roads lead to parking spaces. In the city, the dinner party talk is about how you got there and where you parked. The roads go through neighbourhoods where community group leaders watch anxiously from behind barred windows. They lead from downtown streets, where parking is scarce, to suburban malls, where parking is everything.

If you want to live in a city, the best advice is: Don't get a car; if you have one, get rid of it, trade it in on a microwave oven or a karaoke outfit. You will then be best equipped to observe the first lesson of city living:

How To Beat the Traffic
Walk.

Without a car you will be, at the same time, living somewhat outside the city experience. You cannot talk about how hard it was to get here. You can say: "Just hopped a 52 bus and was here in a flash" – but no one wants to know that. You can't talk about how hard it was to get here and you can't talk about how tough it was to find a parking place. Once, just once, you can say: "No problem for me: I don't even have a car." After that, people will tire rapidly of you. They will leave you out of conversations. They will stop inviting you out.

Some people have responded to this by collecting a great store of other people's parking stories:

"I know a guy, had an Audi, green I think it was. Well, one time he had to be somewhere downtown for nine o'clock and he circled the block and circled the block and circled the block till before you know it, it was 10:30. So he left because he was running out of gas and he lost the contract. Now he always goes an hour early to everything. Isn't that something?"

Those stories lack impact, somehow, particularly if they are about someone who is not in the room. Of course, you could begin making your own stories by becoming the proud owner of an automobile, but what's the point in that?

How To Amaze Your Friends with Parking Anecdotes

Instead, collect parking stories and tell them as if they had happened to you. No one needs to know that you don't have a car, since you had to park it ten blocks away.

If you choose this ploy, always leave well before everyone else, so no one asks you for a ride. Normally, this means missing dessert, but that, and the ten-block walk, will be good for you.

Note: When bumming rides from other people (when your "car" is in the shop), never offer advice as to places to park. City people have developed expertise in these matters, at least in their own minds, and don't want any help.

What If You Are Unfortunate Enough To Own a Car?

1. The best strategy is to park in the first legal place you see. Parking in illegal places costs money and sets a bad

example for courier trucks. If the first legal place you see is an expensive parking lot, so be it. When you arrive at your eventual destination, after walking the twenty blocks, you are poorer but glowing from the exercise. And if you put any value at all on unfrayed nerves, as you should, you have saved a bundle by not having to circle the block ten times and have near fist-fights with guys in Mercedes.

2. Unfortunately our urban society has not advanced sufficiently to honour you for parking twenty blocks away in an overpriced lot. You could make this point, when the conversation turns to parking, how society has not advanced sufficiently to honour you. But people will laugh at you, or resent your superior ethical position. You could lie, make up a hair-raising story about zipping, in reverse, into a tight spot just around the corner, narrowly edging out this big guy with blond hair and sunglasses in a black Mercedes who was going to pull into it frontways, and how the big guy was so mad that he even hung up the phone so that he could make rude gestures at you with both hands.

But that would be lying, wouldn't it? When you find yourself continually lying in the big city, it is time to move out and begin lying in the country, or perhaps the suburbs.

3. Anyway, there is no need to lie. When asked where your car is, simply say: "It's just in a little spot I know," and smile in a secretive way. City people understand. Their life is a continuous search for secret little spots and they don't expect you to betray yours.

As a conversational tactic, being secretive is much underrated. Since the competitive instinct was let out of the cage by Ronald Reagan in 1981, people have expended far too much energy trying to top the other guy in all areas of life, and especially in talking about all areas of life. You can play that game yourself, either by competing frantically to get a bigger this or a better that, or by lying desperately about the size of your income, the cost of your house or the nearness of your parking spot. Or you can stay out of it altogether and keep your thoughts to yourself.

Sometimes this is absolutely impossible, as in the other major area of urban discussion – real estate. All conversations that are not about parking are about real estate, except for those that are about other things entirely. Where do you live? How do you like it? Do you mind if I ask you how much you paid for it? Did I ever tell you about how we found our house? And so on. The point is, you can't stay out of the discussion. You live somewhere, right? You can't deny it. So that means you have to say something about it. All you can aim for is to make sure the topic doesn't stick around too long.

Surviving the Real Estate Conversation

1. Simply saying "I rent" won't do the job. People would sooner talk about buying than renting. They want to talk about what they paid, what somebody down the street paid, and how the neighbourhood is on the way up (only other people's neighbourhoods are on the way down). So there will be a momentary lapse when you say you rent. But eventually someone will ask where, and when you tell them, talk will shift merrily to a comparison of the restaurants in the area.

2. If you own a house and think you did pretty well on the deal, don't make the mistake of saying so. That will trigger at least an hour's worth of anecdotes, bragging, and market analysis. Better to say, "I bought when it was high and sold when it was low," and look sad. People will respect your honesty, see that the discussion pains you and either move on to something else or, more likely, move somewhere else in the room.

3. Or try this: "I don't want to talk about it." That phrase, coupled with the secretive look you learned in the parking section, can convey almost anything – from the fact that you

don't want to talk about it, to the fact that you had a horrible experience that hurts you even to this day, to the possibility that you made a killing and don't want to go into it for some reason, perhaps modesty, perhaps not wanting to give away any secrets.

When you say you don't want to talk about it, people may think you know more than you do, which is all right. Also, you won't have to talk about it. And by refraining from lying and boasting, you will place yourself in a good position in case modesty and truth ever come back into fashion. The way fashion swings, you never know.

How To Be Fashionable

The conventional way to do it is straightforward and expensive:

1. Read newspapers and magazines every day and find out what people are wearing, what music they are listening to, what social trends they are talking about, what restaurants they are going to, what books they are reading, what film directors they are watching, what social trends they are supporting, and what neighbourhoods they are living in. Then buy those clothes, move into that neighbourhood, support that cause, read those books, eat at that restaurant, buy those CDs (unless CDs are out, in which case you should buy that digital audio tape or whatever), and go to those movies.

2. Keep a careful eye on the newspapers and magazines in case any of these things should change.

It is a simple matter, being fashionable, given unlimited time and money. And its importance in city life is huge. Next to parking and real estate, fashion occupies the largest space in the world of urban conversation. Yet, in a way, it is completely overrated. Eighty per cent of the people go through their lives completely and happily unaware of changes in fashion. They may have a vague sense that bell-bottoms arrived and eventually left. They may know that the Beatles existed and then stopped existing. They know that Elvis is either dead or alive. Aside from that, they do what they always do, live as they always lived, wear what they always wore, and eat what tastes good, assuming the doctor will let them. Without knowing what is in and what is out, they can go from being out to being in to being out again without even being aware of it.

Eighty per cent of the people are like that. Ten per cent are fashion leaders and the other 10 per cent are fashion followers. Don't write this down, because there will be a new and more fashionable theory tomorrow.

Okay, so the 10 per cent establish what is fashionable. Eighty per cent ignore it. They wear polyester until it wears out, then buy cotton because polyester isn't available, are briefly in step with the times until polyester comes back and they are still wearing cotton. The other 10 per cent try to catch on to what the fashionable 10 per cent are doing.

But the fashionable 10 per cent keep changing the ground rules. As soon as their fashionable neighbourhood catches on, attracting unfashionable people (the second 10 per cent), they move out. When too many people adopt a certain restaurant, it ceases to be fashionable and is discarded. The colour orange is in, until it begins to be seen in shopping centres; then it is out.

The drive to be fashionable is the race to stay ahead of the mainstream. Because of the power and sophistication of the mass media in spotting and popularizing new trends, the mainstream always catches up, whereupon the fashionable move on.

Given that it costs too much, in both time and money, to keep up and stay up, the real challenge is this:

How To Be Unfashionable and Survive

One way to survive being unfashionable is not to know that you are. You don't worry about your clothes and your music and your choice of restaurants because you are not aware that anyone is judging them. Ignorance is strength.

Unfortunately, it is difficult to remain ignorant enough in the Information Age. The radio and television, the posters on the subways and buses, the newspapers and magazines – all combine to give you a picture of what a person of your age should be like. One day you are waiting for a bus and you see that someone's hair on a billboard looks different; one evening you are listening to the radio and you happen upon a panel discussion about a kind of music you did not know existed. The panelists discuss it knowledgeably, as if they had been studying it in detail for years. Only now it is going out, they say. And you didn't know it had come in. A few such shocks and you are suddenly possessed of the impulse to keep up. The next step is to find out what you are keeping up with. And the step after that is to realize how truly difficult, and necessarily unenjoyable, it will be.

That is when you begin wondering whether there is any way at all you can hang on to your present tastes without sticking out so much that tourist buses make you part of their regular route. What are the options?

1. Choosing the Noble Savage routine, you condemn all that is modern, deliberately flaunt your Dodge, your wide lapels, bell-bottoms, tuna casserole, and Glenn Miller records. This is inexpensive and courageous, probably too courageous for most of us. The plus side: You become known as an individualist. Another plus: No one borrows your car or your records. Possible plus: In a few years, your tastes may be on the leading edge, as fashion begins another loop. Still, not for the faint of heart.

2. Bluffing like crazy, you claim that everyone on the Left

Bank or in SoHo or Chelsea or North Beach is decked out like you are. Advantage: You get to keep your clothes. Second advantage: You may be telling the truth; it is not long ago that the hippest stores on Kings Road were selling old Little League baseball shirts. Disadvantage: You wouldn't be able to keep a straight face. Second disadvantage: Bell-bottoms drag along the sidewalk and pick up all kinds of dirt. Conclusion: It can't work; people can find out what's happening in SoHo at any magazine store. Your only hope is to invent some presumably hip section of, say, Dublin and claim that your look came from there. But the risk of discovery, in the global village, is still great, and it seems a lot more trouble than just going to the shopping centre and picking up a reasonable facsimile of today's look, cheap.

3. You keep what you have, but add to it just one small identifiably avant-garde feature. Your acquaintances will see only the bold stroke, allowing you to keep your Hush Puppies, pastrami sandwiches, and Four Freshmen records.

Example: A perfectly ordinary, in fact rather bourgeois, apartment becomes daring and dangerous if there is a live snake loose in it.

Example: A routine collection of books becomes memorable if it includes a shelf devoted to the Royal Family.

Example: A visit to an everyday restaurant can be a trip to the edge if you taste the Perrier and send it back.

Some of the great city-dwellers of our time – space does not permit naming them, but they know who they are – are not particularly stylish and not terrible fashionable. But no one thinks of that. They think of your doorbell playing that song from *Man of La Mancha*, the peculiar Belgian movie poster, that thing in the aquarium, the way your car alarm talks like John Garfield. Meanwhile, the great city-dwellers go on living their lives, their simple tastes intact, eating macaroni and renting Jack Lemmon movies.

Q. & A.: How To Be a Great City-Dweller, Even in a Small City

To be a great city-dweller, you have to learn to cope grace-fully with some of the institutions of the modern metropolis, some of the laws, written and unwritten. You have to learn how to make friends and make sure they will not betray you to gossip columnists. What follows are some of the most fre-quently-asked questions about city life and some of the ques-tions that are never asked at all.

Q. My neighbourhood association wants me to join. Apparently if I don't, everyone will think my home is a crack house. What should I do?

A. Join, by all means. Even if your home *is* a crack house, joining will help you meet people who can give you tips for decorating it tastefully. And there will be rummage sales at which you can buy books for it cheaply. If your house is not a crack house, joining your neighbourhood association will help you keep crack houses out. Many neighbourhood asso-ciations operate on the assumption that every application for rezoning is, until proven otherwise, an application to operate a crack house. This may seem mean-spirited to those who run group homes and shelters, but it is a fact of city life.

Q. But I will have to do work if I join the neighbourhood association, won't I?

A. Easily managed. Volunteer to count cars. There has never been a case in which a neighbourhood association went to city hall and complained because too few cars were driving through. Every car, as we have seen, contains potential crack house customers. So there is a desperate need for the number of cars to be counted in order that the association can make representations to City Hall. You don't really have to count them. Just put some numbers down. Make them low, if you want to help the group home locate in the neighbourhood. Or make them high if you want to give the association a good fright. The number doesn't have to be too high, since any number of cars is too high. Either way it doesn't matter. City Hall won't accept the numbers. It will do numbers of its own.

Q. I have bought a bicycle and want to know some of the signals most commonly used by bicyclists in the city.
A. You point upwards with your left hand if you are turning right, out if you are turning left. You point up with your second finger if a motorist cuts you off. You put your thumb to your nose if the motorist stops to object to your previous gesture. Then you turn around and pedal off in the opposite direction.

Since you are then going the wrong way, you make a V with two fingers as a gesture of peace toward the motorists who are driving right at you and honking.

After a few such episodes, most city cyclists realize that the best place to cycle is on the sidewalk. This requires a new signal, to be directed at pedestrians who are forced to leap out of the way. The signal consists of rolling your eyes and shrugging your shoulders good-naturedly, in a gesture internationally recognized as meaning: "I know I'm not supposed to be on the sidewalk but you should see what it's like out there with the cars, and I'm sorry you dropped your bag of groceries."

Q. My city only allows smoking in the doorways of unoccupied buildings. I am quitting smoking tomorrow myself, but what should I advise my friends who don't have the will-power?
A. The wave of repressive measures now being directed at smokers is a temporary phenomenon and will recede when those in charge of repression get over thinking that they'd really like one about now.

In the meantime, if you want to get out of the doorways, form a Doorway Smokers Association and apply to City Hall for a permit to smoke in doorways. This will definitely be refused, enabling you to look elsewhere for places to smoke. Mine shafts are good, although not all cities have them. Public washrooms are not bad. They have excellent washroom facilities, and many are close to hotels and bus terminals, but they tend these days to be filled with people using their cellular phones. Much of the outdoors is still open to you, provided you do not exhale. Good luck with your quitting.

Q. How can I make people listen to *my* burglary story?
A. This is one of the most commonly asked questions in the city today. Everyone has a burglary story; many are quite dramatic and yours won't be heard unless it has elements that set it apart from the rest.

For a start, it helps if you did not feel violated. Everyone who has been burglarized feels violated. Men, especially, like to say they felt violated because they think it shows women they are sensitive. If you say you didn't feel violated, people will want to know why.

Then you will have to think of something. "Possessions don't mean much to me," you could say, which is a nice counterpoint to the wails you have been hearing about the loss of priceless furs and state-of-the-art sound equipment.

Having actually encountered the burglar adds a dramatic element to the story. And saying "It's not important" when asked what happened when you encountered him adds the right touch of mystery. You subdued the burglar, or he subdued you. You'd just as soon not talk about it. Either way, it is a more interesting tale than merely coming home from a weekend in the country and finding the vcr gone.

If you actually *knew* the burglar, knew his background, that would count for a lot. Or if you *ran into him on the street* a few months later and got to know him, got to realize *why* he had turned to crime, that would be a fascinating story. Failing that, there is always: "I stared at him and he stared at me. Then he walked by and was gone."

"Why didn't you call the police?" someone will ask.

You give your tired shrug. People love it when there is no reason for what you do. It makes your life like a foreign film. Every time, it beats the story about how slow the insurance company was to pay off.

Q. I've always wanted to live in a house designated as "heritage" but can't afford to buy one. Is there any advice you can give?
A. Your only hope is to have the house where you live now designated. You do this by having someone threaten to tear it down, whereupon you go public with your plea to save this particular piece of architecture from the wrecker's ball. Generally, this alone will get the public and the media so excited that no one will ask how it is that someone else is threatening to tear down a house that belongs to you.

From then on, certain difficulties have to be overcome. If your house is, for example, a split-level ranch-style semi-bungalow built in 1966, it will be difficult to sell city planners on the idea that it is worth preserving from an architectural point of view. You can try, as others have successfully, the argument that it is the "one of the few remaining examples of the Etobicoke School of suburban architecture." In doing so, you will have to list some of the factors that make it unique, or at least partly unique, such as the cold room under the stairs, the stained plywood breakfast nook, and the fibreglass carport.

Even this might fail, at which point your best recourse is to locate historical value in the former occupants of the house. Someone famous may once have lived there. (It is not considered an adequate argument to say that someone famous may live there in the future.) Do not use Elvis's name or any well-known political leader, since these have all been thoroughly researched. But famous dead writers have lived in all sorts of places, and one of them may well have composed a poem or two at the breakfast nook or behind the bar in the rumpus room.

Q. How can I get rid of the religious nut at the door?
A. First, remember that it could be you. If you were a lot sadder than you are now, or a lot happier, you could be going from door to door trying to tell people what you know. Now, how would you feel if you wanted to tell people what you knew and they slammed the door in your face or laughed at you? The other thing is, do you know how much nerve it takes to walk up to a total stranger's door and knock on it, especially if there's a doorbell? Such a person deserves commendation, not scorn.

Q. You've convinced me. How can I become a religious nut knocking at people's doors and do so effectively?
A. Remember that not everyone has read the above. They are suspicious of you and a little frightened, particularly if you have bells attached to your feet, or are walking around in pairs, dressed neatly in dark suits. A key is to recognize that most city dwellers are, first of all, frightened of strangers and, secondly, suspicious of anyone who seems to have deep convictions about anything. So your best strategy is to be frightened of them too and shy to the point of wanting to take flight. When they answer the doorbell, thrust your pamphlet into their hands, saying, "Please read this. I hope you don't mind," then turn as if to rush away. Such a show of vulnerability may cause them to lose their fear and express some interest, as a way of comforting you. Then you can lay the pitch on them, being careful not to look them right in the

eye. If your strategy has not worked, at least you are halfway down the walk before they can begin cursing at you.

A more devious strategy, one that only the boldest will attempt, is to carry a kitten with you at all times and pretend that you have just found it and seek to return it to its rightful owner. It is not easy, once in the door, to switch the conversation smoothly from cat chow to God's Plan, but you must have learned how to do that by now.

Q. I can't get into my house half the time because I don't remember what numbers to punch to get past my home security system. Plus my car always thinks I am trying to steal it and squeals whenever I try to unlock it. What can I do?
A. Many city dwellers have discovered that the secret to peace of mind and a feeling of security is getting rid of security systems.

Q. I've figured out that the only way to beat the traffic and get to the cottage for the long weekend is to leave on Thursday after work. Are there any good new excuses for leaving a day early?
A. Surprisingly enough, the best excuse is still the sick uncle. A mainstay of the Forties and Fifties, the sick uncle fell into disuse in more recent times because it was thought to be hackneyed and unsophisticated. In its place arose a new set of excuses involving such things as psychoanalysis, the position of the stars, and bad combinations of drugs. With the expansion of major-league baseball, various short-term excuses emerged, used only for rare afternoon games. The computer figured prominently in these, as in: "No point in me hanging around this afternoon. Calgary's computer is down."

By now, technology-generated excuses have become all too familiar to management. Meanwhile, psychoanalysis, astrology, and drugs have lost their currency. But no one has used the sick-uncle routine in years. Because the latest generation of managers is schooled to be supportive and empathetic, your request to take Friday off is unlikely to be challenged. No modern manager is going to say: "I *bet* your uncle is sick, you lying little sneak." In fact, if your manager says that to you, you can probably raise it with the office Employee Morale Co-ordinator.

A note: Some employees, wanting to be considerate, have tried to schedule their sick-uncle days off well in advance.

"Excuse me, but I just found out that my uncle is going to be sick, so I wonder if you could let me have Friday off in six weeks, just at the start of the Labour Day weekend."

Don't try this unless you work in certain federal government departments.

Q. Some aspects of city life are very frustrating, such as when planes are delayed. I know that people are supposed to take out their frustrations by yelling at the person behind the ticket counter, even though it isn't her fault. But the line-up to yell at her is usually too long. What can I do?

A. Yell at the people who are yelling at the person behind the ticket counter. It isn't her fault after all. Sample dialogue:

Outraged passenger: "This is ridiculous! I won't stand for this! Why is this plane always late? I absolutely *must* be in Winnipeg by seven!"

Second outraged passenger: "That's right! I bought my ticket two months ago and now you say the plane is late! What are you going to do about it?"

Third outraged passenger: "Stand aside, I can show even more outrage than that, and since I'm only dealing with a clerk I feel particularly courageous! Get this plane going right now or I'm going right to the president on this!"

You: "Stop yelling at her! Can't you see it's not her fault! Grow up!"

Now, this won't get the plane going or satisfy your urge to punish the airline. But it does satisfy your urge to yell at someone, doesn't it? And without hurting innocent people.

Q. I have always wanted to be a street character because every few years they get human-interest stories written about them in the newspapers. What are the current requirements?

A. The prerequisites for street characters are continually shifting, as you imply. At the moment, street characters should not appear to be poverty-stricken or homeless, so as not to upset middle-class newspaper readers. If homelessness cannot be avoided, it should be made clear that the street character has *chosen* homelessness and prefers it to any other way of life. A neat appearance is useful, as well as the avoidance of ranting. Today's model street character makes absolutely no sense, as it is traditionally understood, but speaks quietly and sounds reasonable, so as not to disturb the tourists. He or she walks along the street while talking, rather than standing in one place. Religious topics should be avoided, but some political content is allowed. A sample:

"Of course, they'll never admit it, right?, but there's no way, no way, they didn't know what they were doing when they put the taxes up. You think the Queen wasn't consulted? You think the Pope wasn't in on it? Get real, my friend. Everybody knows, but the media keeps it a secret. And why? Well, did you ever think it might have something to do with the weather we've been having? Did you think it was a *coincidence* that it didn't rain today but rained yesterday? And where was the prime minister? Exactly."

There is no money in being a street character, it should be pointed out. A street character keeps on the move and can lay down no guitar case in which to collect coins. People only become street characters for the love of it. However, now is not a bad time to become one, although you should hurry up about it. Soon cities will be licensing street characters, in an attempt to keep too many of them from congregating in certain downtown areas and at the same time provide street characters to suburban streets that are lacking them now.

Chapter 5

Suburbia Today:
Breezeways without guilt

How To Commute by Car
How To Commute by Bus and Train
At the Mall

City dwellers endure smog, traffic, overcrowding, noise, and crime. And sometimes it bothers them. At those times, their only consolation, the only thing that makes their lives worthwhile, is the thought that others are worse off. And where are the others worse off? In the suburbs.

It is an article of faith that life is miserable in the suburbs. The word "'burbs" has become a guaranteed laugh line for stand-up comedians – like "bagel" or "reefer" or "7-Eleven Store": All they have to do is say the word and audiences break up. In from the 'burbs for a night out on the town, suburbanites laugh too, in self-defence. For years now, they have taken it as a given that their lives are pitiable. They have apologized for where they lived, muttered some excuse about how they happened to be where they are, promised to move soon, either downtown or out into the country. Of course, it is easier said than done. Once in the suburbs, people are likely to stay out in the suburbs. It is time they began to stop feeling sorry for themselves. It is time they fought back.

If you, for some reason, find yourself in the suburbs, the

first thing is to face squarely the attack from your downtown friends. What do they say when they come to visit? They say they can't find the place. So? *You* can find the place. And there's something to be said for having a place not everybody can find.

Then they say it's so far away. From what? From smog, traffic, overcrowding, noise, and crime. Well, and some restaurants. But hey, there are restaurants in the suburbs, even ethnic restaurants. And when you come right down to it, the suburbs now have their own crime, brought to them by criminals who can no longer afford to live in the slums, now that the slums have been bought up and renovated by young stockbrokers.

So you've got crime, you've got restaurants. What else? You've got a basketball hoop over the garage door and nobody downtown has that, because nobody downtown has a garage, except for some dinky falling-down thing at the back of the property that isn't regulation height, and as for apartment buildings, forget it.

You can park your car on the street without a permit, which you don't have to do anyway, since you have a garage and a driveway. Your friends can easily park on the street outside your house when they come to visit. And you know what that means: it means that suburban conversations are not about parking. They are about not being able to find your house, but at least it's something different.

Now it's true that your street is probably named after a tree. It may be that the tree is usually found in the Caribbean. Worse, your house may be in a subdivision where all of the street names begin with the letter R. But you should not accept too many cheap shots. Downtown people are beginning to emulate you, you know. They barbecue downtown too. They have lawn ornaments, even when they don't have lawns.

Q. What do you respond when a downtowner asks how you can live out here when the commute is so terrible and you're putting so much exhaust into the atmosphere every day?

A. Easy. Say: "I know, I know. I just couldn't afford to live downtown. I simply refused to get into that real estate hysteria. I really envy you where you are, but . . ."

The implication, a good one to nudge out onto the playing-surface, is that the downtowner is into that real estate hysteria up to his eyeballs. And since the average downtowner lives in mortal fear that he will find out he bought too high or sold too low, the suburbanite has hit him in a vulnerable area.

Q. My friend, who lives downtown, says the city is a better place to bring up children than the suburbs. I am offended, though somewhat soothed by the fact that I can park my car without a permit. What is my rejoinder?

A. The city argument is that children downtown are close to museums, concert halls, and arenas, and that they meet a greater variety of children. However, since children spend all their time hanging around strip malls, the argument doesn't amount to much. Suburban children, instead of hanging around mere strip malls, can hang around huge shopping centres, which offer a great variety of stores, actual fountains, and free concerts by quite good amateur choirs at Christmastime.

While the average downtowner views crime, congestion, and a certain amount of dirt as inevitable byproducts of the vitality of urban life, he wonders, in the dark night of the soul, whether he is doing the right thing for his children. He remembers, from when he was growing up, the kinds of neighbourhoods Donna Reed's children lived in, and Ozzie and Harriet's. They weren't like this. This self-doubt is another area of vulnerability at which the besieged suburbanite can aim.

Downtowner: "Don't your kids get bored?"

Suburbanite: "I guess they might sometimes. But I feel safe with them out here. I like to see them on their bikes, riding around the neighbourhood, through the parks. I sort of expect to see Beaver Cleaver come riding around the corner any minute."

This is called "playing the Beaver Cleaver card" and is to be done sparingly.

Of course, the fact that you can win debates with your downtown friends does nothing much for the quality of your life. You still have to face the commute, the shopping centre, the schools, the minor-hockey association, and that green imitation-wood panelling in the TV room.

How To Commute by Car

1. Have a good tape deck in your car. Never listen to the radio. The radio will tell you which routes to avoid. Everybody will try to avoid them, causing other routes to be congested. The radio also broadcasts the news, which will just annoy you, and the time, which will worry you.

2. Never change lanes. Decide at the outset on an inside lane and stay there. If you make up your mind never to change lanes, you will not grow envious of the people in the next lane who seem to be moving when you are not. Eventually, your lane will be moving and theirs won't and they will be envious of you. Deciding that you will move faster in another lane is just inviting a broken heart down the road.

3. Above all, love and understand the other drivers. If you enter the commute with the idea that other drivers are jerks who want to cut you off or tailgate you as they gesture with the hand that is not holding the phone – if you enter the

commute with that sort of idea, you will arrive at work each day with your stomach in a knot and a heart full of hate. Remember always that other drivers have problems too: Maybe they have trouble at home; maybe they are racing to the hospital; above all, maybe they will die young from ulcers and high blood pressure caused by trying to beat the traffic all the time. When you encounter a person like that, jumping in ahead of you at the last minute before a lane ends, or tail-gating you and gesturing in anger, smile and wave. He will be made even angrier, poor fellow, by the fact that you are happy. Soon, there will be one less car on the road.

How To Commute by Bus and Train

1. The most acceptable form of commuter conversation is none at all. There is no point taking any chances. If you are soaking wet, it is acceptable to say "Wow, it's really coming down" to your seatmate as you sit down. If someone says "Wow, it's really coming down" to you, it is acceptable to grunt, keeping your head down in your newspaper. Always have a newspaper or some form of reading material for keeping your head down in. (Note: In certain regions it is more acceptable to talk to strangers, and strangers will not regard you as a pervert should you say something pleasant to them on a bus or in a train. It is wise to check the local regulations before venturing onto public transport.)

2. If you are a rookie bus rider, you are likely to be enthusiastic about the service and proud of yourself for leaving the car at home and protecting the environment. It is not wise to share any of these thoughts with fellow passengers, most of whom take the bus because they have to and may not think of it as fun, exactly.

3. On the other hand, you may be unpleasantly surprised by how long you have to wait before the bus arrives. Probably it is the result of a delay caused by a car driver such as you would have been had your vehicle not been in the shop. Since

it is not the driver's fault, the fact that he happens to be the sole representative of the transit industry available to hear your comments does not entitle you to lecture him on the shortcomings of the service, especially if you only began using it today. You are, however, allowed to mutter once you reach your seat, provided no one is listening.

4. If there is no seat and you are required to stand, it is probably not the end of the world, although it might seem so for a time. A good technique for getting a seat is to stand near someone who would be expected to give you one, in a polite society. Since it is not a polite society, there is no point standing near a high school student. High school students are healthy and strong but need their rest. Also, they don't see you. Old men are invariably polite, and if you stand near one, he may give up his seat for you and make you feel terrible.

5. A feature of public transportation is the presence of twelve-year-olds who offer loud demonstrations of new words they have learned. You could lecture them on some aspect of living as you have learned it, but what would be the point? Better that you decide you didn't hear it, then accept it as part of the rich tapestry of modern life.

6. There is nothing wrong with giving up your seat for an older person or, if you are a man, a woman, especially if the woman is carrying packages. If the woman is not carrying packages, she may suspect you of ulterior motives. Knowing this, you may hesitate to give up the seat, not wanting to insult her in any way and because you are comfortable sitting down. This is something you have to work out for yourself. If you do decide to give up the seat, it is not acceptable to hang around, hoping to bask in gratitude for your noble gesture. Just give up the seat and move to the back. It is not as if you risked your life for her or anything.

7. The Law of Subways: If this train is so full that you can't get on, the next one will be so full that you can't get on. You can fret about this, or you can shrug and wait for the next

train, which you won't be able to get on either. Eventually you will get there. This fact is worth repeating, as an important piece of knowledge about life in and around the city: Eventually you will get there, even from the suburbs.

At the Mall

Most of us are used to malls by now. We take them for granted. Yet they are fairly new to our society; there have been few studies done of the sociology of the mall and hardly any attempts made to provide us with codes of behaviour. This lack may be due to the fact that, for a long time, people hoped that malls would go away. Wishfully thinking that the mall was a temporary phenomenon, we decided that there was no point in getting to know anything about them. We were wrong.

In the past twenty years, the period in which the mall has taken over North America, we have accumulated some knowledge about malls. It is as follows:

1. With the exception of where the fountains are located, every mall in North America is the same as every other one.

2. Mall designers always hide the washrooms.

3. There are no clocks in malls, except in jewellery stores, where they always say it is ten minutes before two o'clock.

4. People driving cars in mall parking lots are at their lowest point, in terms of displaying the better human qualities.

5. Small children always want to go to malls and always cry as soon as they arrive.

There are some regional variations, most of them relating to smoking regulations and fast-food availability. In the more sophisticated parts of North America, such as Ontario, smoking is now confined to a small designated area of the fast-food section. This has confused teenagers, who recognize that there is no point in hanging out somewhere you can't smoke. Hanging out in shopping-centre doorways does not seem fun, particularly since it means hanging out with grown-up smokers. How this will be resolved is difficult to foresee, but clearly a major social change is on the way. Either teenagers will stop smoking – a slim probability indeed – or they will begin hanging out outdoors – a slimmer probability – or they will begin hanging out in vacated premises such as mine shafts and downtown stores.

Since the merchandise available in all malls is the same, the only identifiable local characteristic is the smell coming out of the food court, the smell that eventually comes to permeate every corner of the mall. Since different varieties of pizza are popular at different points on the continent, that is how you can tell where you are: by what the pizza smells like.

With the above facts in mind, it is possible to compile, for the first time, the Official Guide to Mall Behaviour:

1. Park as far away as you can. No one will fight you for the space and the walk will do you good.

2. Tell yourself: "I am not in a hurry."

3. Watch out for people who are in a hurry and stay out of their way.

4. Never put yourself in a position where you have to find a washroom. Malls hide them. If you go to the Information counter to find out where one is, you will have to line up behind thirty people who are buying lottery tickets.

5. Remember that one factory in Korea makes all the handicrafts sold at malls.

6. Never eat anything blue.

7. Wear a watch. That is the only way of knowing if it becomes night all of a sudden.

8. Christmas begins the day after Hallowe'en.

9. Don't stop and stare at people videotaping their children sitting on Santa's knee. It is normal behaviour. If you think it's weird, you're not normal, OK?

9. Valentine's Day begins the day after Boxing Day.

10. Easter begins the day after Valentine's Day. Valentine's

Day candy can be bought cheap and given for Easter, but don't try it. People are too smart to fall for that.

11. You can't buy a baseball glove during baseball season. At the mall, hockey season begins when school is out. The time to buy a baseball glove is in March. There may be something available in May, but only if you are left-handed.

12. Keep telling yourself, "I'm not in a hurry."

13. Back to School starts the day after Easter.

14. Be aware of disoriented people who don't know what time it is, what season it is. They may also fear that they have spent too much money and know that they have just spent two hours in the company of crying children who wanted to eat something blue. For all these reasons, they want to get out of the parking lot before you do, and they don't care much what they have to do to accomplish it.

15. Look on the bright side: You are not in a hurry, you're left-handed, and you haven't eaten anything blue.

And when you get home, you won't have any trouble parking.

Chapter 6

In the Country (the green area just behind the mall)

In the years ahead, more and more people will be moving to the country. There are two main reasons for this:

1. Life in the city.
2. Life in the suburbs.

Technology will be behind it – or, in this case, ahead of it. At last, the long-promised electronic cottage will begin to function. Workers, physically isolated from the workplace, will actually be able to work using long-distance lines and computers. Everybody knows all about that. The newspapers have been predicting it for more than twenty years. Until now, however, the setting up of the Electronic Cottage foundered on the rocks of the boss's paranoia. The boss figured that if workers could not be seen, they would probably be up to something unproductive; if allowed to work at home, they would be washing the car on company time.

Somehow, that distrust has broken down, in large measure because the boss has retired and been replaced by one who actually *likes* technology. Now the workers are moving out of the office, their space being taken up by employee-relations consultants and larger photocopiers. It is no small irony that just as management is spending millions to find out how to make the workplace more enjoyable for workers, the workers are moving out of the workplace altogether.

Those who are moving out of town because they don't need to go to the office to work are joined by another group: those who are moving out of town because they no longer work at all. The same technology that enables some jobs to be done from home enables some other jobs not to be done at all, or to be done by computers. This is also thanks to the Information Age.

Many of those who received the information that the Information Age had taken away their work decided to leave the city behind, since there is not much reason to be there if you don't have to work in it. Further, a person without a job stands a better chance of warding off starvation if he lives somewhere where it is possible to lift potatoes out of the ground and tomatoes off a tree, or wherever they come from.

This is the attitude that many city people bring to the country, which is why the years ahead are going to be rather tense, in terms of people getting along. Lately, there have been disputes in both Ontario and British Columbia that foreshadow some of the difficulty lying ahead. City people, newly moved to the country, threatened to take their farm neighbours to court because their cows made so much noise and their fields smelled of manure.

Clearly these were people not quite prepared for the move out of the city. As the Information Age brings city and country people closer and closer, we will have to work together, the city people learning what it is that a tomato grows on, the country people learning to recognize the difference between an Electronic Cottager wanting to live the country life and a developer wanting to pave the countryside.

Where Is the Country, Anyway?

Usually, there is a big fence at the back of someone's suburban yard. Beyond it are no buildings. That is where the country begins. Sometimes it is found behind a shopping centre. In the country there are trees and cows and gophers. Some of the roads are not paved. In the fall, there are hunters in the fields, in the winter, snowmobilers. Stopping the car and getting out of it, you will notice a different smell in the air, which takes its flavour from the absence of grease and automobile exhaust. These are some of the tell-tale signs of being in the country.

Some day you may take a wrong turn out of a shopping centre parking lot and notice, after a few minutes' driving, that there are no Mexican restaurants, no used-car lots, and only an occasional video store. You are in the country, and will be in it until you see the first signs of the next city, consisting of German car dealerships, giant waterslides, and billboards announcing hotel chains and adult contemporary radio stations.

Not all country looks the same, but all country shares the characteristics mentioned above. Almost all, anyway: at some point, you may be walking in what appears to be countryside except that you seem to be continually threatened by small vehicles driven by cursing men wearing brightly coloured trousers. If this is your situation, you are not in the country; you are on a golf course and should leave immediately.

A word of warning, however: the line dividing the country from the city and suburbs is constantly shifting. Developers, ever on the lookout for empty space upon which to build malls, parking lots, amusement parks, and golf courses, send lawyers out into the country in search of farm owners who have decided they have now lost enough money that they can call their agricultural career complete. As a result of this process, new shopping centre parking lots appear at the back of old shopping centre parking lots. But there is still country out there, at this writing, and it looks pretty much as it always has.

Not all country is fields and trees. There are towns and villages in the country, distinguishable from suburbs by the fact that they have main streets, big old churches, farm-implement dealers, and a relative absence of strip malls. People who live in such communities do not all get up and go to the city every day, although there is, increasingly, some of that. Certain tell-tale signs make it possible to recognize rural communities that are being infiltrated by commuters:

1. White frame houses painted blue.
2. Old brick houses with decks.
3. Restaurants serving escargots.
4. Tennis courts.

Generally speaking, the closer a small town is to the city the more likely it is to have businesses with evocative rural names such as General Store and Farmers' Market. A country cousin of such communities is the cottage-country town, in which 75 per cent of the downtown businesses are antique stores and 40 per cent of the shops are called shoppes.

Country is also, as bad poets have told us over the years, a state of mind. But the differences between the country state of mind and the city state of mind are continually narrowing, thanks to television, radio, video stores, and other agents of the Information Age. Country people are exposed to pretty much the same cultural influences as city people. In one sense, that means country TV has as many car chases as city TV; in another sense, it means that city sound systems play just as many songs about trucks as country sound systems. Still, there are differences. Perhaps the most important element in the country state of mind is that people in the country are closer to the country. So that's what they think about, and that's what they talk about.

Coping with City People

When people from the city enter your rural world, they could be bringing good things, such as friendship. Or they could be bringing bad things, such as money. As a concerned citizen of the country, it is important to recognize the difference. Some city people, call them settlers, want to become your neighbours. They are retirees, hobby farmers, and electronic cottagers. Other city people want to pave your neighbourhood. Here is how to tell the difference between a settler and the lawyer for a developer.

1. The lawyer will be friendlier.
2. The lawyer will have a telephone in the car.
3. The settler will be falling in love with the soil, reaching down occasionally to grab and smell handfuls of dirt. The lawyer will ask if there is a place he can wash his hands.
4. If your visitor wants to know where the nearest school is, it's a settler. It's a lawyer if he wants to know the location of the nearest Land Titles Office.

If you find out that your visitor is one of those who wants to pave the land, your obligation is clear: it is to confuse him. There are tried-and-tested methods all city people recognize as authentic because they remember them from asking for directions or from seeing a Walter Brennan movie.

How To Confuse a Developer

Some country people, when confronted by a smooth talker from the city, try to compete on the same level. They demonstrate how well-read they are, how up on current affairs, how much they know about life in the city. It is not hard to do nowadays, in the Information Age (not to mention the Global Village). But it is a mistake. The smooth talker, sensing a worthy adversary, gets his guard up, becomes smarter and more devious. Before you know it, there will be a golf course where the next farm used to be. Better not to play on his turf.

What will put him on the defensive is his lack of understanding of country ways. If you don't have any country ways, this is the time to invent some. The smooth talker won't recognize the difference.

1. Do the mumbling, drawling hillbilly bit. "Shucks," you say, picking up a stem of grass to put in your mouth, "folks around here don't hardly never cotton on to stuff like that and such nohow." Confusing enough in itself, the sentence is particularly effective when used as an answer to the question: "How do I get to the Land Titles Office from here?"

2. If standing outside, sniff the air suspiciously, lift your foot, and glance askance at the sole of your shoe. People from the city are at a distinct psychological disadvantage when they fear they have stepped in something.

3. If the telephone appears from the car, marvel at it and ask if you can use it. Then phone a friend: "Guess where I'm calling from," you say. "Standing right outside the barn, over by the tractor. This lawyer feller's got the durndest phone contraption you ever seed." The lawyer will beam – and your friend will sound the alarm around the community.

Lending a Helping Hand

Once you understand that your new neighbour is someone who wants to escape the city rather than bring it to your doorstep, it is time to lend the helping hand that country people are famous for. You are probably cursing the person, whoever it was, who popularized the fact that country people always lend a helping hand. Always having to lend a helping hand makes it tough to take naps, or enjoy the birds and other supposed benefits of rural life. But there it is. Someone needs help and you have a reputation to uphold.

You can't be half-hearted about it either. You can't wander over and mumble something like: "Looks like you folks have everything pretty much under control. I came over to see if you needed a helping hand, but since you obviously don't, I'll just be moseying along."

That is not the spirit that is bringing thousands of potential settlers out from the city every year. If the migration continues, you might want to trade it in for a different spirit, but for the moment you have to remember that you're famous for the helping hand. Remember, you're not giving up the helping hand forever. You're just lending it. Furthermore, in lending the helping hand, you can take the opportunity to offer guidance that may benefit you in the long run.

1. The settlers may not actually want to grow anything. This is to be encouraged, rather than sneered at. Who wants someone else's livestock wandering over your land? Especially pigs and chickens. Also, if your neighbours are not growing anything, they won't be asking you for advice on that. Sometimes a little dissuasion is possible. Note that here you don't need your mumbling, drawling hillbilly voice:

"From what's been happening with the GATT, it looks like growing nothing is the best strategy for the moment. Of course, it might change in a couple of years if the government adjusts intelligently. But it won't hurt to wait it out for a couple of years instead of rushing into pigs or chickens or something like that."

2. City people will quickly try to talk the way they think you talk. This consists mainly of putting extra prepositions and adverbs into everything. Try to keep them from embarrassing themselves and they will thank you eventually:

City people: "Well, we all were just right passing by and thought we'd drop on over and up and see how you all were doin' and every little thing."

You: "That's very nice of you. We were just having a glass of iced tea. Why don't you join us? We were just saying that we'd love to hear what you think about what's happening in urban architecture these days."

3. If you have livestock and your new neighbours give indications that they will, now that they are country people, take up hunting, help them familiarize themselves with the differences between the things they can shoot and the things they shouldn't.

City people: "Hidy. We was just over on hard by the Seventh Line and we thunk we might up and drop by to chew the fat some."

You: "Glad to see you. Why don't you come in for a dry martini. We were just looking at some photos of cows. See, here's one. Notice how it doesn't look at all like a deer."

4. Since you know about wiring, helping them to set up their expensive stereo system will give you the opportunity to make the point about how well sound carries in the country, particularly after dark. (If you don't know about wiring, make sure you learn. All country people are supposed to know about wiring and fixing cars. It is amazing that they let you live out there without knowing.)

How To Talk to Settlers

Much depends on whether you want them to stay or not. Some former city people can make a big contribution to life in your part of the world. Others immediately want to establish ballet classes, two-year-old kindergarten, men's drumming groups, and other city fixtures. Many such people can be persuaded that they really miss the city around the seventh time a pig wanders into their kitchen. Assuming, for the moment, that you want to be a good neighbour – it is written somewhere that country people *have* to be good neighbours – you must learn the art of conversation with an exurbanite. More than subject matter is at issue here. There are certain responsibilities you have in holding up your end of the conversation.

1. Be unspoiled. Most city people have come to the country because they are sick of urban values and want to think

the country has not yet become infected with moral rot and lite pasta. You will not make your new city friends happy if you are as cosmopolitan and cynical as the friends they left behind. Say you get up with the sun, even if you don't. Say the dessert came from a bake sale at the church, even if it came from the supermarket.

2. Be wise. This is expected of rural people. You should know how to fix things, or talk as if you can. You should know what grows, and whether it is a tomato or a potato. The settlers, even if they don't actually farm, are going to want to put a little garden in. Of course, not all country people are handy at everything. But it is cruel to disillusion settlers who have come a long way, given up friendships and a way of life. They didn't come all this way to find out that you don't know what tomatoes grow on either. Fortunately, lack of wisdom can be concealed through the timely use of rhetorical questions.

Settler: "We thought we'd put in some potatoes."

You: "You thought you'd put in some potatoes?"

Rare is the settler who will dare follow that up. Difficult questions about mechanical things can be dealt with in a similar way:

Settler: "I wonder if you could give me some advice on the pump."

You: "What's wrong with it?"

Sometimes that alone will do it. But the alert settler may respond with something like: "It doesn't work." Your response then can be: "What part of it doesn't work?" None of that is too helpful, of course. But you can then recommend someone who really does understand the pump and still convey the impression that you know what you're doing.

You: "Well, I could give it a try, but I'd hate to mess it up. There's a guy in town I know who is a lot better at it than I am."

3. Be sentimental about your farm. Your new friends don't

want to hear about what a burden it is, how you can never get away from it. Worse, if you are really doing well, your new friends *certainly* don't want to know about it. They want to know how you do it all for the sheer love of it, your love of the animals, the smells, the dawn, the soil, the fertilizer, the machinery in the barn, the barbed wire. On the other hand, just because your farm is immensely profitable is no reason to lie about it:

New friend: "I guess it's not always easy making ends meet."

You: "All I know is, I'm going to stay on the land no matter what."

4. Where you live is "the land." It is not, say, "Exactly ninety-five kilometres southeast of Edmonton." The people who left the city did so because they wanted to live on "the land." Don't disappoint them.

5. Remember that city people have certain expectations about how you live. They want you to be a gallant participant in a vanishing way of life. Be gallant whenever you can. This does not just mean opening doors for people or helping them over puddles. It means gritting your teeth and murmuring about "the banks." It means remembering the Dirty Thirties and dust, and when the trains used to stop in the next town and the mail used to be delivered six days a week. If you can't remember the Dirty Thirties, it would help if you could remember someone who remembers the Dirty Thirties.

6. The vanishing way of life comes in handy when it comes to defending pursuits, such as hunting and snowmobiling, that are scorned by city people. "It's what we've always done on the land," you say, adding, "and I hope we can keep doing it for a few more years."

Coping with the Country

Before you can begin to cope with country people, you have

to cope with the country itself. That means, for a start, getting used to some of the city things you no longer have.

1. Parking, at least as a topic of conversation. In the country, you can put your car just about anywhere. If you raised the subject at dinner, people would think you were crazy.

You: "One thing I've noticed about the country is that you can park just about anywhere."

Other people: "Whaaaaat?!?"

You have gained a parking space – probably more than one, in fact – but have lost a preoccupation. Don't immediately begin looking for a replacement. It will come.

2. Certain kinds of stores. Most stores in country towns are oriented towards selling goods that people wear or use for something. A lot of city stores are not like that. They sell items that are not used for anything in particular and that you can't wear, but they *define you.*Some shoppes within a fifty mile radius of the city have things like that, but if you go into a store beyond that limit asking for something that will define you, you are likely to meet with puzzled expressions. Maybe they will think you are painting and sell you some masking tape so that you can cover yourself with it and not get any paint on you.

This will change, as television and magazines convince small towns that they need to have boutiques in them. Perhaps by the time that happens, you will have found another way to define yourself.

3. Restaurants where the guy carries the giant pepper grinder from table to table. In country restaurants it is thought that every table should have its own pepper.

4. Cable television. City people who have learned to watch television by pointing the remote control at the set and running up and down the dial, checking out what is on on forty or so channels, will have to learn how to watch television all over again in the country. Country television falls into two categories:

a. Over-the-air television, received by means of an antenna set on a high tower. Each change of the channel requires a concomitant adjustment of the antenna by means of a second remote control, in order to make sure the tower is pointed the right way. After a few weeks of trying to tour the dial in such a manner, the settler learns to watch television the way his ancestors did – by leaving it on one channel and falling asleep in the chair.

b. Satellite TV. For this, a large dish-like object is positioned in the back yard and pointed up into the sky, where there are three hundred or so channels drifting around. The settler reads a TV guide the thickness of a telephone book in an attempt to ascertain what's on and soon falls asleep in the chair without watching anything.

The effect of this is to change, somewhat, the nature of country conversation. In the city, people have conversations which are about the fact that they never watch television because there's nothing good on. In the country, people don't bother to say that they never watch television because they never watch television.

5. Theatre, opera, nightclubs, art galleries, the symphony. These are aspects of city life that city people say they would miss too much to ever leave the city. Having left the city, they find that they don't miss them as much as they thought they would because they never went to them when they were in the city, although they felt good knowing that they were there.

6. The roar in the background. City people don't realize how much noise the streets make, even when the city is quiet. When they arrive in the country, they find they can't sleep. There is no constant hum, so that when an occasional noise arrives, brought by a nocturnal squirrel, say, or the wind, it wakes them up and causes them to worry about elephants crashing about in the living-room.

7. Small dogs.

On the other hand, you will be surprised, perhaps even a little dismayed, at the number of city features that have made it into the country. You likely will not miss out on many flavours of ice cream, which is good. You likely will not miss out on the latest movie about lethal weapons, which is not so good. And because people listen to the radio, the attitudes of the big-city talk shows find their way into country conversation, for better and worse. You would be unwise to suspect your new neighbours of not knowing what's going on in the rest of the country, the constitution, the new books.

Answering Your Most Common Questions about Country Life

Q. I've just moved to the country and heard this rumour that oats, wheat, and barley are different from each other. I thought they were all just breakfast-cereal jargon. Is this something that should concern me?
A. Don't worry about it. It's a technical sort of thing. Just keep your mouth shut about it and if anybody raises it, change the subject to the weather.

Q. Why are people in the north so friendly all the time if they don't have any jobs because the mill and the railway are laying everybody off?
A. The reason they are so friendly and nice is that they don't have very much and so they aren't afraid that you are going to take it away. In the city, people have CD players and German cars and worry all the time that they are going to disappear. They would like to be nice to you but cannot afford to take their eyes off their cars in case someone tries to steal them.

Q. Is there a polite way to persuade snowmobilers not to drive across my lawn?
A. You could say, "Would you mind not driving across my

lawn?" This often works, unless the snowmobiler has his helmet on at the time and his motor is running. Another way is to hand him a note saying, "Howdy, neighbour. I noticed you crossing my lawn the other day and was so happy you didn't break through the ice into my new heated duck pond."

Q. I don't have a gun. Should I be ashamed of that?
A. No reason to apologize. No reason for anyone to know.

Country friend: "I guess you'll be shooting those groundhogs, eh? What are you using?"

You: "Actually, I hate to frighten the dogs. I have this whistle that sounds like a groundhog spouse pleading with the groundhog to come home for dinner in the middle of the river. I think I'll try that. Shame to waste good ammunition on a groundhog."

On the other hand, there is no reason to feel superior either.

Wrong: "I don't see any reason to have a gun around. I have better ways of asserting my masculinity."

Also wrong: "I hunt groundhogs with a camera."

Right: "I'd love to go hunting with you but I have to work on the damn tractor."

Also right: "I'd love to go hunting with you but it's my day to cook."

Contrary to what you might have heard, this last works pretty well. It marks you as a non-conformist, someone who is not afraid to tell the truth. If you feel the need, you can add the phrase ". . . and I have to go strangle some chickens."

Q. Every farm I've ever been at, there are eight kittens lying around. What is the origin of this and should I get some kittens too?
A. Cats were believed by the early Romans to be good luck in warding off mice. At every farm you've ever been at, there are actually nine kittens lying around, a number suggestive of

the nine lives of a cat. You must have missed one somehow. There is no particular reason for you to have kittens lying around your own place, as long as you don't mind continually having to answer the question: "What happened to your kittens?"

Chapter 7

At the Table: The new rules of competitive dining

What If You Can't Cook at All?

How To Survive a Healthy Diet

Speaking of Food

How To Break Up a Food Conversation

A Note on Wine

How To Break Up an International
Food Conversation

How To Have Dinner with Country People

Mysteries of the Mystery Dinner Unlocked

How To End the Mystery Dinner

More than ever, we need to know how to dine. Dinner is more important now than in the past. And it will be more important in the future, even if all we are eating is pills made out of seaweed.

Dinner used to be about eating and talking. Television destroyed that. Dinner became something to do while you watched the news. The joy of eating was experienced vicariously, watching happy people happily eating in the commercials.

That was it for the joy of eating and the joy of conversation for many years, until about a decade ago when someone – probably a cookbook author – discovered that dinner and conversation could be combined into a recreational activity. As we have learned, that meant dinner would become solemn and competitive.

As a competitive event, dinner used to be concerned only with using the proper fork and surreptitiously getting spinach out from between your teeth. Now, however, dinner tests other aspects of your personality:

1. How good you are at cooking.

2. How healthy you are about eating.

3. How good you are at talking about food.

For many of us, brought up to eat quickly whatever was on our plates without thinking about it too much, then push back our chairs and clear the table so as not to miss the ball game, the challenge of competitive eating is daunting. And it is not likely to go away, since dinner has an enduring quality as one of the few activities that does not require us to go out in traffic. People will be eating, and talking about eating, for years to come. We must learn how to cope.

What If You Can't Cook at All?

If you are a woman, it's quite all right. You have more important things to do and are courageously blazing a trail away from traditional roles. Just buy something, plunk it on the table, and talk about the elegant take-out place where you got it and how difficult it was to park there. Or, if there is a man around, wait for him to do something. The moral high ground is yours and it is only a question of how hungry you are.

If you are a man, you have a problem, which has about four possible solutions, some riskier than others.

1. You can lay your cards on the table, tearfully confess that you never learned, that you had a mother who did everything for you and that you have deeply resented her ever since.

2. You can play the buffoon card, lurch about the kitchen in a well-meaning way, making self-deprecating remarks as you drop things on the floor, mistake the flour for the sugar, and wait for someone else to take over.

3. You can find out the name of her elegant take-out place and drag back something from there, looking preoccupied and explaining that you somehow couldn't *face* cooking tonight. This will help give you the image of someone for whom cooking isn't everything, which is quite accurate as it turns out.

4. You can play the noble savage. This, the riskiest strategy of all, involves portraying the guy who doesn't believe in all that kitchen stuff and who would, if local bylaws permitted it, be out there hunting and gathering. Hostility and ostracism are the risk you run, but there is a chance that in some circles you will be tolerated – even fed – as a curiosity, an example of a vanishing breed.

How To Survive a Healthy Diet

Some people actually enjoy living on salads and lentils and bean sprouts and whatnot. But most people don't, yet are constantly faced with the necessity of coming to grips with mysterious green (and sometimes black!) things on their plate. It is not likely that the trend will reverse itself rapidly. New seaweeds, ferns, roots, and mosses are being discovered every day. Your strategy is only a holding action. You want to avoid (a) having to serve the stuff yourself, and (b) being invited back.

In deciding what to serve, the doctrine of political correctness can be turned to your advantage:

1. Placing a platter of spaghetti and meat sauce on the table, you say: "I had my heart set on couscous but the only lentils they had were from Iran."

2. When the pizza arrives, you say: "I've been rethinking my position on vegetables after reading about the situation of migrant farm workers."

As for making sure that you are not invited back for another healthy platter of unidentifiable plants, the proper remark should do the trick.

a. "Tofu makes me fart."

b. "Once I had a salad just like this only somebody put poison ivy in it by mistake. For a month, every time I swallowed it itched like crazy."

c. "On the radio the other day they were talking about how plants cry when they feel pain."

    d. "Guy I knew in school was a vegetarian. It got so extreme with him that he couldn't look at a cow without throwing up."

Speaking of Food

Conversation at the table is now exclusively about food. The recent trend to murder-mystery dinners is, in a way, an off-shoot of that: it means that the hosts have no confidence in their ability to talk about food for an entire meal.

But most hosts are not like that. The meal will begin with a discussion about the soup, typically with the guests invited to guess the mystery ingredient. You have two options here, depending upon the degree to which you want to ingratiate yourself with your hosts. If you want to be invited back, you guess something extremely exotic, such as Tibetan sycamore root. If you think you might never want to be here again, you guess salt. The beauty of picking salt is that it the cook imme-diately wonders if he put too much salt in the soup – the most basic of culinary flaws – and spends the rest of the evening on the defensive.

The meal continues with a discussion of the main course, the spices, the identity of the more unusual-looking ingredi-ents, and the place where the dish was first encountered. Invariably that will be a foreign country. If the dish is low in cholesterol, that will be pointed out. If the dish is not low in cholesterol, it will be described as "sinful." (Some people reserve "sinful" for desserts, but the accepted term for des-serts is "decadent.")

In calculating our ability to survive such a conversation, it is worth remembering that the conversation will be much longer and more detailed if a man did the cooking. Routine attempts to change the subject, with comments such as "How about those Expos?" and "Do you think there's any alternative to the total extinction of the human race?", will not work. But some techniques will.

How To Break Up a Food Conversation

1. Say: "Do you have any ketchup?"

2. Get up in mid-course, excuse yourself, and, looking a bit uncomfortable, leave the table for about twice the usual amount of time. Flush the toilet twice. On returning, toy with your food and say: "This is very nice."

If this works, the game is not necessarily won. The danger is that the conversation, while shifting away from this particular meal, will stay on food. It will become a great-meals-I-have eaten discussion. (Our conversational patterns are more and more peculiar. Watching a baseball game, people will talk about other baseball games. Sitting at a table eating veal, people will want to talk about sitting at other tables, eating fish.)

If you want to get into this yourself, there are certain hints to keep in mind. First, don't pick an obvious country – France, for example: everybody has eaten in France or, more likely, eaten with someone who has eaten in France. Pick a country where it is unlikely that someone has had an excellent meal – Cambodia, for example, or England. Extra points are available for omitting all mention of country and simply referring to a region.

"There was this blowfish on the Algarve, I remember. It was just before the season, so the house white was particularly ingenuous . . ."

A Note on Wine

No one talks about wine any more, at least not the kind with corks. The proper style is to put the screwtop bottle on the table, with the price sticker still on it. If there is to be any discussion, it will be about how you got it cheaper in this little suburban strip mall. In the future, there will be discussions about what goes with pills made out of seaweed – red or white?

How To Break Up an
International Food Conversation

Not all people can participate easily in food discussions. Being unaware in early childhood of how important food would be to them later, they probably had many memorable meals at which they were not paying attention. Their impulse now, on hearing the great discourse about major international culinary adventures, is to break up the conversation, or break away. Several avenues are open:

1. Follow the discussion of that nice little three-star place on the Rhône with your detailed description of the great donut at the Husky station just on the edge of Sault Ste. Marie.

2. Politely interrupt someone's speech about the curried goat in Delhi and ask where the TV set is. People are polite. They will always tell you where the TV set is.

3. Ask: "Has anyone here ever had monkey?"

How To Have Dinner with Country People

1. Don't expect a lot of talk about the food. Someone may ask "What's that?" if you put one of your gourmet meatless things on the table. After you tell them it is adapted from a little Greek thing you learned about on the local news in Toronto, there will be a silence and then someone will talk about the weather. Food in the country is regarded as more for eating than for conversing about.

2. Still, it is permissible to talk about the weather. Make sure you know the forecast and can remember what the temperature did the past few days. In the city, weather means whether you open the window or not. In the country, weather matters. It even matters to you. If things are getting too dry or too wet, it makes a difference. When someone comments on five consecutive days of rain and you say you hadn't noticed, you make yourself sound very foreign.

3. Adopt an attitude, even if it's hard for you, of complete humility. No matter how much you have learned by listening to radio programs about the joys of going back to the land, you cannot hold up your end of any conversation about cisterns, wells, pumps, cows, or tractors. Bluffing is just silly:

You: "I've noticed that most of the cows around here have the same colour scheme."

Country person: "Uh, yes? Who do you think's going to take the Booker?"

Attempts to gain advantage by exploiting your more cosmopolitan lifestyle will not work either:

You: "You know, tractors in Europe are quite different from what we've got here."

Country person: "What have they got there?"

Uh-oh. Now you have to make intelligent, comparative comments on North American tractors versus European ones. It is not enough to say they have more blue ones in France.

That is why the only safe course is the humble course. You don't know about tractors. Say so. Ask some questions about tractors. You don't know about wells. Ask. People love to lend a helping hand.

4. Resist the temptation to suggest ways for country people to improve their lives. Maybe a modem would make a big difference in the way they do business. Maybe they'll figure that out for themselves when the time comes. Maybe you're just showing off.

5. Remember that food is food. Learning to talk about vegetables should not be too hard. Tomato and potato are quite different and once you get the hang of it, you'll never forget. Zucchini and squash look kind of the same, but no one's going to think less of you if you get that wrong once in a while. Everything comes out of the ground, so if you learn to say a few things about the soil, you are in good shape.

Remember that some of the vegetables you thought of as real delicacies in the city are used to feed the hogs in the country, and try not to be too shocked. Remember also that in discussing vegetables you don't want to get too philosophical:

You: "There's something about the, oh I don't know – the *roundness* of a ripe tomato in the morning sun that makes me think about the richness of existence."

Country person: "They start tasting pretty bad if you let them sit too long without eating them."

6. Don't be too romantic about animals. You will see foxes, groundhogs, raccoons, deer, weasels, maybe even a bear. Gushing over them doesn't show how close to the land you are. Country people see those animals all the time and most of them are pests in one way or another, interfering with either crops or livestock. Country people tell great stories about animals, which will enable you to tell whether you should regard them favourably or not. If you are not sure how to regard an animal, you can trigger one such story with a neutral type of comment:

Wrong: "We saw a deer last night. Aren't they beautiful creatures?"

Right: "Another deer came through the yard last night."

Mysteries of the Mystery Dinner Unlocked

Who knows why mystery dinners happen? It may be that you have finally triumphed and your hosts have settled on the mystery dinner as a way to avoid talking about food. (Why they still want you at the table is a mystery in itself. Perhaps they still enjoy the company of your spouse.) It may be that they have been reading magazines again to find out what to do. Or it may simply be that somebody gave them the game for Christmas and they want to try it out. Since you have shown yourself to be pretty bad company under ordinary circumstances, they figure that you might be more enjoyable to have around if you are playing someone other than yourself.

The details vary but the main idea is the same. You receive in the mail a card announcing that you are to appear for dinner disguised as an Argentinian polo player who is afraid of heights. Your spouse is told to portray a silent film star whose feather boa was purchased wholesale. For days you practise your Argentinian accent and your spouse says you sound like Inspector Clouseau. Your spouse says you are being a bad sport by insisting that a polo shirt by Ralph Lauren will be enough of a costume. So on the afternoon of the dinner you are forced to drive to Woolco and purchase an entire stupid croquet set, though you live in an apartment building, simply so you will have something to carry.

Meanwhile, your spouse, unable to find a feather boa anywhere, has ripped open a pillow and is glueing feathers onto your old college scarf. The apartment is a mess, your throat is sore from trying your Argentine accent, which now sounds like Howard Cosell, and your spouse is not saying anything at all, except in subtitles, carried from room to room on a yellow legal pad.

You are in no mood for dinner when it comes. Your mood is even darker if you are a man and have to wear the feather boa, or a woman and have to wear gaucho chaps, swing a croquet mallet, and talk like Inspector Clouseau.

But you keep telling yourself that tonight, at least, you will not have to talk about food. When you arrive, you find your hosts, who seem to be Harry S Truman and a female lumberjack with a scarlet letter A fastened to her back with Velcro or something. There is a man whom you recall insulting once over a three-bean salad and he seems to be a pirate, although he has a budgie on his shoulder. His wife is not there, but there is a woman with him who is wrapped in sheets and talks like a faith healer. One of you murdered somebody.

The fourth couple, complete strangers to everyone, apparently, are both in drag. She may be a football player, although she is wearing a bicycle helmet, because she says things that sound like a garbled version of what Vince Lombardi might once have said. "When things get going tougher," she says upon being introduced, "I get going too." Then she asks her husband if she has it right. The husband looks quite fetching as the French maid, although his accent sounds like Howard Cosell.

A sinking feeling descends upon you as you realize that this will go on for at least four hours, following which you are likely to be stopped by the police on the way home and have to stand beside the car wearing a gaucho outfit and holding a croquet mallet. Before that, every time you try your Argentine accent the French maid is going to think you are making fun of him, your spouse is going to knock a lamp over with the feather boa, and the budgie is going to fly low over the soup course.

How To End the Mystery Dinner

Is there a way out? If your hosts know the game well, probably not. They will know that nothing can be revealed until the very end of the evening. But it may be their first time (nobody does it twice), so you have a chance with one of the following ploys:

1. Confess, even as soon as the soup is on the table. "I can't lie about it any longer," you say as Anthony Quinn and Howard Cosell. "I did it and I am prepared to accept my punishment. There, I feel a great weight passing from my shoulders. Pass the salt, please."

2. Pretend to be the victim. After having eaten enough to dull the hunger pangs, collapse at the table, a victim of "poisoning," and insist, for realism's sake, that you be removed from the scene and carried away, preferably to the room where the TV is.

3. If neither of these ploys works, compliment the host extravagantly on the soup and say that you tasted one almost as good on the southern peninsula in early spring a few years ago. Either the conversation will now switch to great-meals-I-have-eaten (not so bad now that you think of it), or else your host will have to respond as Harry S Truman, which could be diverting for at least a while.

Chapter 8

Home: A place to hang your head

How To Live in a Family
(If You Don't Have Any Other Choice)

Junior's First Book

An Alternative to Taping the Flying-Up Ceremony

What To Do If You Accidentally Tape Over Your
Mother and Father's Wedding Video

Remote Control: Better than no
Control at all

Nintendo Love

Tape That Binds

No matter how much the world changes, certain institutions remain. They change too, but they endure. We are talking about the family, the school, the government, the church, the bank, the tavern, the hospital, the video store. In a turbulent world, they offer stability and a place to get out of the rain. What lies ahead for these important institutions, and does it matter and blah blah blah and all that?

How To Live in a Family
(If You Don't Have Any Other Choice)

Home, as an institution, is in a transitional phase. Strange things go on now, true, especially around the stereo and on the bottom shelf of the fridge, but it will become stranger still.

To drive this point home, it is only necessary to note that the family of tomorrow begins today with a complete video-tape of the wedding day. By the time tomorrow's teenagers are born, their parents will have lived at least thirteen years in a household in which the most important day of their life sits in a box under the VCR, between a copy of *The Revenge of the*

Pink Panther and an instructional video about hitting long irons for better accuracy.

How many times will they have watched it by the time their children become teenagers and what effect will it have had? How many times will the teenagers have watched it and how will it affect their views on love and families?

We can only speculate, and we will. For many people, the wedding day is the only day of their lives that is recorded and preserved. There may be a snippet of a hockey game or a birthday party here and there, but they have probably been recorded over. The wedding is there in great detail, from trying on the veil to flinging the garter. What that tells our bride and groom is that nothing before or after the wedding day is of much consequence. If they have married young, it means they have long lives ahead of them containing nothing worth videotaping.

It is not difficult to see in the weekly trip to the video store a symbolic attempt to recapture that moment of happiness and importance. And it is not difficult to see how unfulfilling it must be to return, not with cameras flashing and confetti in the hair, but with the second-most-recent *Police Academy* picture and a large package of red licorice.

What a change from having one's every move recorded; the guests, hundreds of them, ordered about so as not to detract from any shots of you; the (optional) cloud of dry-ice smoke swirling around the floor for your first dance together; the camera- and (optional) sound-persons hurrying to stay ahead, like a CNN crew; the bandleader making sure that only those who should be in the picture, according to the script, are on the dance floor.

And later, watching in the privacy of that first home, laughing at the bridesmaids and wincing at the best man's speech, the one it was promised would be edited off the video because it did sort of make the thing look bad. And some more years later, seeing the slender people up there, dressed so well, looking like the "After" pictures in the TV commercials instead of the "Before." And later still, forgetting about it and bringing it out only when the in-laws insist and marvelling at how *you* could be the centre of attention, that so many people, not to mention a camera and sound person, could be so interested in everything you did.

What lessons are learned from this, and conveyed to the children? That the wedding is more important than the marriage? That people will pay attention to you, even videotape you, if you follow the script – eat when it says, smile when it says, dance when it says. That an event is not important unless it is recorded for posterity?

Who can know? But the number of rituals in our society is increasing – graduations from kindergarten, elementary school, dog obedience school, assertiveness training; awards ceremonies of one kind or another; closing banquets, ribbon-cuttings, prom nights. The rituals enable the videotape cameras to be brought out and the big day to be preserved for posterity – or at least a spot on the shelf underneath the VCR.

In the modern age, family events have to be watchable. Pressure increases on children to do things that can be videotaped. This is bad news for those who hoped that today's children would *read* more than yesterday's – unless the event can somehow be ritualized.

Junior's First Book

Fade in on Junior, putting on his new reading outfit, while Mom and Dad stand beside him and smile.

Dad (speaks to camera): Junior, I am proud to say that you have now reached the age where you are ready for your first book.

Junior (speaks to camera): Thanks, Dad. And I would like to thank Mom too, for helping to get me ready for this day.

Mom (speaks to camera): Well, what are we waiting for? It's time to climb the Book Ladder.

Junior ascends the Book Ladder and takes down from the book-case a book that is marked with a piece of red ribbon. He looks at it and smiles, then speaks to the camera.

Junior: Mom, Dad, thanks! *The Catcher in the Rye*!

Dad: Son, both your mother and I had our first reading experience with that book and we wanted you to share it too.

Junior descends the Book Ladder and hugs his mother, then sits in the Reading Armchair and opens the book. Dad turns on the Reading Light and shakes Junior's hand. Junior takes a deep breath, then begins to read. Grampa walks in and stands behind Junior's chair with his hand on Junior's shoulder. Junior's lips move slightly. Mom and Dad and Grampa wave at the camera, as we

FADE OUT

The ritualization of family life poses challenges to family members that their ancestors never had to face. If Cynthia Flies Up on the same night as Dad's Forty-and-Over Touch Football Wind-Up Banquet and there is only one video camera and Dad is the only one who can run it, there is bound to be strain. When the first ten minutes of a movie about lethal weapons appear on the videotape right where the first ten minutes of Mom putting on her veil should have been – well, there are problems here that our forefathers and foremothers never had to face. Their lives were troubled only by drought, starvation, and the Axis powers.

An Alternative to Taping the Flying-Up Ceremony

Get Cynthia to take detailed notes on her feelings at the time. Then Dad can record her speaking those feelings into the camera when he gets back from the Forty-and-Over Touch Football Wind-Up Banquet.

What To Do If You Accidentally Tape Over Your Mother and Father's Wedding Video

Call your grandmother and borrow her copy. Have a duplicate made. In the unlikely event that your mother and father actually want to see the wedding video before the copy is made, say that you loaned it to a friend who has a sister who is getting married and you wanted her parents to see what a truly great wedding looks like.

If your parents actually see the lethal-weapon movie taped over the first part of their wedding video, announce that you are running away from home. This will trigger the following sequence of events:

1. Your mother will forget about the wedding video.

2. Your father will jump into the car and drive to the corner store to pick up blank videotape.

3. When he returns, you will all study the Running-Away-From-Home Video Suggestions that came with the camera.

4. You will be videotaped packing your suitcase while your mother stands tearfully by. Then you will be taped walking out the door carrying your suitcase and hugging your brothers and sisters, if any.

5. Before you run away down the street, you will be handed the camera by your father, so that you can take a shot of your parents waving at you as you run away. (In fact, you will walk backward slowly, so as not to cause too much jiggle in the shot.)

6. You will run back to your home, hand the camera back to your Dad, then run away for good.

The modern family differs from its predecessors in so many ways that it is difficult even to count them. This is too bad, because modern people like to quantify things, like to be able to say: "The modern family differs from its predecessors in 193 ways."

Modern families don't have a Mommy and a Daddy and 1.7 children. They might have their original Mommy and a second Daddy and one of Mommy's kids and two of Daddy's, which can be seen, alternatively, as the original Daddy and a second Mommy and two of Daddy's kids and one of Mommy's. Or they might have two Daddies and no kids at all, or two Mommies. Or one of the kids might have been brought there by a surrogate Mommy instead of by the traditional stork. Advances in biological science being what they are, there is probably a surrogate stork available if necessary. It is possible to buy greeting cards for surrogate mothers now, which shows that the free-enterprise system has sanctioned the whole thing. And this means that, no matter how complicated the modern family gets, it will always be possible to send greeting cards to it. There will always be a Mother's Day, of sorts, and a Father's Day, even if it only honours a test tube.

That is encouraging. It brings a reassuring kind of continuity to an institution trying to muddle through a crisis of identity, wondering how many people are supposed to be in it, as well as whose kid that is and why the wedding video is showing the first ten minutes of a violent adventure movie and where to find the remote-control unit in order to get through the machine-gun fight and on to the cutting of the cake.

Remote Control: Better than no Control at all

That is another difference between today's families and the families of yore: Today's families cannot operate without certain small machines, remote-control units, that are easily lost. A sociologist would say that the rise in importance of the remote-control unit symbolizes the remoteness of the family, the loosening of ties, the growing sense of alienation in family life. That's the way sociologists are, always offering some damn theory, never stopping to help find the stupid thing. The modern family faces extinction because remote-control units keep getting lost and all sociologists can do is walk by muttering about alienation.

In the days of such pioneers as Ozzie and Harriet, when there were two children, one Mommy, and one Daddy, and the next-door neighbour was always in the kitchen helping himself to the last piece of cake, there were no little machines. The television set was a big thing in the living-room with knobs on the front. The telephone was in the kitchen, attached to the wall. The garage door opened when you lifted it. The record player worked when you turned it on and the record dropped and the needle moved over onto it.

Nowadays the next-door neighbour could not get at that piece of cake without tripping some sort of electric-eye thing that would cause a silent alarm to ring in the nearest police station.

Policeman: "Did you hear something?"

Second policeman: "No."

First policeman: "Must be one of those silent alarms. I wonder if the next-door neighbour is into the cake again."

But that is not the point. The point is, the CD player needs a remote control pointed at it to work. So does the television. So does the VCR. So does the garage door. These are handy devices because they enable us to do things without having to stand up and move around. Standing up and moving around would make us like our forefathers and foremothers and we couldn't have that. According to the advertising, a million horrible things can happen to you between the car and the garage door if you have to get out of the car to open the thing by hand. So far there does not seem to be too much that could happen to you if you had to move between the couch and the television set, but you never know. It's true that the next-door neighbour is hardly ever in the house any more, but there could be gremlins and aliens and whatnot. In short, you need that little thing.

The question is, where is it? That's what is rending families asunder these days, and the problem will only intensify in the years ahead as science comes up with new devices, such as the toothbrush that runs by remote control. It is true that the prospects of a remote-controlled toothbrush seem pretty remote, but there's no stopping science. Certainly if your teeth were not located in your mouth, it would make sense to sit across the room from them and brush them by remote control.

Anyway, that is not the question, which is, as you remember, where is it? What seems to have happened is that somebody drove in, opened the garage door, closed it, took the garage-door opener into the house, and put it somewhere. So nobody can take the car out. Meanwhile, the remote from the TV is under something, so nobody can watch television. And everybody in the household denies watching television and being in the car, particularly after that episode last week in which somebody drove down the street changing everybody's channels, which is said to be a technical impossibility. Still, how can you be sure when that television set comes on every day at 1:37, puts itself on Channel 2, then turns itself off a minute later. Clearly, there is a Greater Power, and the Greater Power may have a remote control too.

The disputes that take place over such matters are intense, more intense than those of twenty years ago. Granted, those disputes were, in a way, about the same thing: You can't take the car, and you can't watch television. But they were about whether you were *allowed* to take the car and *allowed* to watch television. Now, allowed or not, you can't, because the little thing is gone. Maybe somebody went to make a sandwich and left it in the fridge.

Q. It has been suggested to me that getting rid of all the remote-control devices in our house might eliminate the irritants that make family life so tense. Is there any sense in this?

A. Your question reveals a longing for simpler times. The sad fact is that the number of things that you can turn on and off, open and close with your hands is diminishing rather than enlarging. This reflects a growing trend towards people wanting to do things from across the room, a trend that bodes ill for the continued survival of the human race. An alternative, worth thinking about, is getting rid of all the things that the remote controls operate. That would mean no television, no vcr, no garage door. You will find out that it is possible to live without all of these. The question is whether anyone will want to live with you while you are finding out, particularly if thieves walk into the garage and take the lawnmower.

Nintendo Love

Given the remote quality of family life, the tendency of family members to do everything from across the room, there is a real question as to whether love, as we have traditionally known it, can survive in the context of the modern family. The quality of remoteness is intensified by something we haven't mentioned yet, the tendency of the modern, technological family to play games by remote control. The Nintendo sits in the family room and Mommy and Daddy, Sis and Junior and other family members, such as Second Daddy and Previous Mommy and StepSis, sit there and move controls around, shouting and becoming emotionally involved with cartoon figures moving around the screen.

This in no way resembles sitting around the piano singing Stephen Foster songs, the way we are told our ancestors did. On the other hand, maybe the ancestors of our ancestors

figured everything was going to hell because of all the singing of Stephen Foster songs going on. Maybe the ancestors
of our ancestors thought our ancestors should be doing what
they did, namely sitting around the harpsichord and skinning
rabbits, or whatever it was. The point is that no generation is
completely satisfied with what its children do.

Still, Nintendo seems a bit much. Given the new domi-
nance of the remote control in our lives, it is not difficult to
imagine Mommy and Daddy lying in bed with their remote
controls, watching cartoon characters bounce up and down
on the screen across the room, making little cartoon gasps
and eventually, if the mood is right, winning a free game, or
perhaps even multiple free games.

Love could come to that. On the other hand, there are
signs that traditional love does endure, in a non-traditional
way. Putting technology to work for them, the children have
learned how to express love in a modern manner. They do
that by making tapes for friends, special and ordinary. It is a
time-consuming process, involving searching through
record and compact-disc collections for individual songs that
are the total favourites of the person doing the taping, putting those songs totally onto a single cassette tape so that that
loved one totally gets a portrait of the music that is important. Tough decisions have to be made. Should the taper play
to the expressed likes and dislikes of the tapee, or should the
taper be totally honest in putting forward his or her music?
What if the tapee totally hates the tape, or at least the B side
of it? Does that mean the relationship is doomed?

Tape That Binds

Certain tensions around the house are caused by the use of
audio tape as a means of romantic expression. For one thing,
it means that the stereo is always in use. It may not seem to be
in use. There will be no one in the room listening to it, but it

will be on, maybe with the volume off, but with technologically impressive lights flashing to indicate that something is
happening.

This is, as you might have suspected, another symptom of
the Remoteness Syndrome. People under a certain age do
not ever sit in the room where the stereo is located and listen
to something. What they do is put something on it, turn the
volume off, set up a tape to record what is on it, and then
leave the room, perhaps the house. Whether the tapes thus
produced are ever listened to is not for people above a certain
age to know, but the practice is common among younger
people, important to them, and not to be smiled at. It should
be kept in mind, however, as a distant threat: the threat that
music, as something to be listened to, may become extinct,
and live on only as something to be preserved and duplicated.

Music is rarely heard in the house any more, although it
exists in, pardon the expression, record numbers. Occasionally an automobile goes by with what may be music playing in
it, so music may not have disappeared altogether. It may just
have adopted, like the expression of love, a different form.

Between parents and children a bond of tape can exist as
well. Because people are so busy these days – or think they
are – it is no longer possible for parents and children (or even
parents and parents) to sit down together to listen to favourite music or watch a favourite television program. That had
been, in past years, the way in which parents conveyed their
tastes and their comedy to their children, and the way children attempted to involve parents in their current choices.
Now it can no longer happen. It is the Information Age, the
Age of Leisure and all that. There is no time.

Child: "Dad, listen to this. You'll like it. It's the Barenaked
Ladies."

Dad: "I used to like barenaked ladies when I was younger
but right now I have to make seven phone calls, load more

paper into the fax, reset the clock on the microwave, see what the Weather Channel says about next Tuesday, pick up your StepSis at computer camp, and something else I can't remember right now but I think I memoed myself in the laptop. Maybe some other time."

Child: "I'll tape it for you."

Dad: "Thanks. If I'm not around, call me at the office and put it on my message where to find it."

Weeks later, Dad will eventually find the memo he faxed to himself concerning the tape and listen to it in the car, between phone calls. He will make a note to tell the child that the tape was great. If he has a few minutes, he will try to videotape the PBS special on Ernie Kovacs in order that the child can see what he thinks is funny, the child being unable to watch it with him because the child is over at a friend's house, preparing a music mix for an upcoming party.

There is no doubt that the members of the modern family– Mom, Dad, Second Mom, Junior, Sis, Uncle Harry, and StepSis – love each other. The evidence is all over the house, on tape.

Q. Last night my husband and I had a wonderful candlelight dinner, then went to bed anticipating a pleasant night of sex nintendo. Unfortunately, my husband couldn't load the program, even when I tried to help him. He said that this had never happened before. I told him it could happen to anyone but he was inconsolable. I am worried about him and about our marriage. Is there something I can buy?

A. It is typical of the malaise that governs our age that you would assume that the key to ending your husband's miseries is something you can buy. What about ordinary common decency and kindness and understanding? Try having him avoid alcohol and abstain from computer activity for a few days. Another possiblity is a black negligee program for your Nintendo.

Q. I want to tell my girlfriend that I love her but I haven't got a tape recorder. Is there any hope for me at all?
A. In pre-tape-recorder days, lovers used to communicate their feelings by talking, by sending flowers or chocolates or poems. You might want to try one of those options. Obviously, some of them require you to be there in person, which is not everyone's cup of tea in the modern age. However, you could fax over a poem or courier some flowers. Some courier services are very fast and you should have your answer within a day or two.

Q. Every day my television set turns itself on at 1:37 p.m. and stays on for a minute. Then it switches to channel 4 and shuts itself off. What does this mean?
A. Your TV set loves you.

Chapter 9

At the Bank: Take the cookie and run

If the family has become a remote institution, dealing with life from across the room, the bank has become even remoter. Its preferred way of dealing with life is keeping it outside the door.

Outside the door is where the bank machines are. Banks prefer to have their customers deal with machines. Then the banks can deal with the machines, getting the machines to pass on the requests that the customers make to them. That way the banks never have to deal with people at all, except in one special way that we will get to later. The system has not been perfected yet: there are still customers who try to deal with human beings at the bank, but more and more people are turning to the machines. They like the machines, they say; you never have to wait for them.

Any bank customer realizes that more human beings work at banks than ever before, despite the increase in the number of machines that are supposed to do the work of human beings. This is in line with the experience of all offices – that labour-saving devices create more labour. So it doesn't really,

at first glance, appear to make economic sense for the banks
to put so many machines outside the front door.

However, economic sense is not the only kind of sense
there is. As institutions, the banks have a long history, with
much to be ashamed of. Over the years, customers have been
snubbed, stiffed, swindled, shut down, and probably several
other things that begin with "s" – all so that banks could pros-
per. Now emerging as caring institutions as the century
draws to a close, the banks are suddenly ashamed of their past
behaviour. Trying to appear open and friendly, they cover the
walls with balloons at the slightest excuse, put out coffee and
cookies for the customers, and dress up in Hallowe'en cos-
tumes even when it is not Hallowe'en.

This necessitates some attitudinal adjustment on the part
of customers accustomed to the traditional behaviour of
banks. Older customers remember that banks did not like
handing out money. In order to get money from a bank, you
had to face a steely-eyed teller, hand over a withdrawal form,
and wait for the teller to get an even steelier-eyed supervisor
to initial the form; then you had to wait while the teller
unlocked the cash drawer, took the money out, and carefully
counted it. Now a machine does all that, not steely-eyed at
all, at least as far as you can tell with a machine, asking you no
questions (other than those you can answer with numbers)
and dropping the money down a chute, wrapped in a sleeve
of paper and not counted out by any human hand.

Borrowing money was worse than withdrawing it back
when banks were banks. To borrow money you had to be
ushered, in front of everybody, into the office of a person,
almost always a man, who was even more steely-eyed than
the people who authorized your withdrawal. As you walked
toward the office, your shoes clicked noisily on the marble
floor and everybody looked at you, knowing where you were
going and why. There were no carpets in banks. And your

shoes did not have soft soles. You would never dare enter the bank wearing soft soles.

You would be asked, upon reaching the office of this most steely-eyed personage, what your reason was for wanting to borrow money. To say that you wanted to borrow money because you needed money was to admit to moral inferiority. You would be warned that there was a penalty you would have to pay for borrowing money and that penalty was called the interest rate. You signed the papers, accepted the guilt, took the money, and walked quickly out.

In the lending of money, the modern bank bears no resemblance to that steely-eyed institution of old. Interest rates are used as a lure to *encourage* customers to borrow money. Pictures of red convertibles and rakish sailboats are plastered all over the walls, in the spaces not occupied by balloons, as an incentive for customers to borrow money.

This is the framework in which you, as a bank customer, must operate. Can you, dealing with the modern bank, keep your dignity and yet still get the money? It is one of the challenges of the modern age.

How To Find a Human Being in a Bank

It is not enough just to walk up to a teller and announce you want to withdraw $75. The well-trained teller will tell you (that is why they are called tellers) that you can complete your transaction just as easily by going to the machine. The teller may smile when giving you this information; tellers are now hungry for human contact, and in their loneliness they take advantage of every opportunity that comes up. But, still, you will be directed to the machine. There are only a few ways around this.

1. Announce that you want to borrow money. Banks, as noted above, now *like* to lend money, and they have not yet devised a machine that will lend money. Several prototypes

have been constructed, apparently, but each was deemed to have eyes that were too steely. If you say that you want to borrow money, you will be put in touch with a human being. After asking a few general questions about the interest rate and repayment schedules, say that you have changed your mind and would like to withdraw 75 bucks.

2. Ask a teller for a balloon for your child or extra cream for your coffee. Few banks have cream machines. The teller will attempt to find some for you. "While I'm here," you say when the teller returns with the cream, "I might as well withdraw 75 bucks."

3. Say that the machine is broken. This will cause a teller to smile because tellers don't like the machine either, and it will cause a flurry of activity among the supervisors, during which you and the teller can have a little chat and perhaps you can withdraw 75 bucks. In the end, you will be informed that the machine is not broken and that you were at fault for not using it correctly. But you will have enjoyed some human contact and you will have your $75.

How To Avoid a Bank Loan

Sometimes, unavoidably, a person simply does not want to borrow money. Perhaps the person has, for the moment, enough money. Perhaps the person's religion prohibits the borrowing of money. Perhaps the person doesn't like the idea of paying interest rates. Whatever the particulars, there are at least a few valid reasons why a person would not want to borrow money. You may be such a person. Yet your bank insists upon your borrowing money. It displays posters depicting the wonderful things you can buy and do with borrowed money. Sometimes it puts actual new cars in the bank. The bank has pamphlets for you to read while you wait for a person or a machine, showing how easy the loans are to repay, how low the interest rates are. Contrary to historical practice, the bank not only tells you that you are not a bad person if you borrow money, it suggests that you might be a bad person if you *don't*.

Let's pretend that you have just entered the bank to withdraw $75. There is a red convertible, a shiny new one, parked inside. You help yourself to a coffee and take a cookie, which you munch while waiting for a teller. After going through your routine about how the machine is broken, you get your $75, thank the teller, decline a balloon, and are just on the way out the door when you are stopped by several bank employees in suits who demand to know why you are not borrowing money today.

This is not an easy situation. You do not want to hurt the bank's feelings, because the bank certainly could hurt yours if it felt like it. Plus, everyone is so friendly. Thinking quickly, you say: "Not today, thanks. I have some money, and anyway I might want to borrow some later."

This turns out to be a mistake. If you understood modern finance, you would have known that. Your chance of borrowing tomorrow is *better* if you borrow today. If you have not borrowed money, the bank doesn't trust you, because the bank doesn't know what your record is like at paying it back. So if you really want to borrow tomorrow, you'd better borrow today too. If wanting to borrow tomorrow is just an excuse, then you need a better one.

You: "I'd love to stop and borrow some money, but I have to catch a bus."

Bank: "Oh, then you'd certainly be interested in our Catch-a-Bus Loan, designed for busy bus-catchers like yourself."

You: "Well, the thing is I already have a lot of debts and I don't want to add any more."

Bank: "A lot of debts? That's excellent. It makes you well qualified to take on another loan. Isn't there something you always wanted that you could borrow some money for right now and purchase right away? Peace of mind, perhaps?"

You: "Peace of mind would be nice, but I can't see where I am going to have more peace of mind by putting myself further into debt."

It is at this point that little warning bells are going to go off in the heads of the bank officials. The use of offensive phrases such as "into debt" could brand you as one of those subversive types who should not be allowed to take advantage of the bank's generous loans policy. Of course, if you want to play the subversive card that's your business. It will certainly get the bank off your back. But the long-run consequences are not good. You may actually need to borrow money some day. So there must be another way:

You: "I really have to be going."

Bank: "You mean, you're not going to borrow money at all?"

You: "I'm afraid not."

Bank: "Not the Red Convertible Loan? Not the Catch-the-Bus Loan? Not the Peace-of-Mind Loan?"

You: "Sorry."

Bank: "Not even the Putting-the-Kids-Through-University Loan?"

You: "No."

Bank: "What about the What-the-Hell-Let's-Just-Blow-It-on-Something-Frivolous Loan?"

You: "Not even that."

Bank: "There must be *some* kind of loan we could interest you in."

You: "Well, I was rather thinking of starting up a small business of my own."

Bank: "Now you're talking. What kind of small business did you have in mind?"

You: "I was thinking of a loan company."

Bank: "Oh, is *that* the time . . ."

Protocol of the Bank Machine

Those who are regular bank machine customers know the etiquette:

1. Stand five paces behind the person using the machine.

2. Pretend not to be watching him, even if he is causing the machine to beep.

3. Avoid loud conversation, which may break the concentration of the machine user, causing mistakes and delays.

4. Avoid eye contact with anyone.

5. Above all, avoid laughter. This is a serious business, an interface between a person and his money. There can be nothing amusing about it.

Defeating the Machine

Your turn comes and you approach the machine, checking over your shoulder to make sure that no one has moved to within four paces. You punch what you think are the right buttons and the little envelope containing the money doesn't come out. Lights flash, beeps beep, and the machine gives you a message: Your transaction has not been completed. The people behind you are beginning to show signs of restlessness, or so it sounds to you. You hear feet being scuffed, you hear murmuring, you hear muffled laughter. Your ears redden. It is a good thing you are wearing your tuque, although it is hot in July. Your every instinct is telling you to run, to get away from this machine, to find a quiet and cool place somewhere deep in the forest. But what are your real choices?

You could walk away, but your card is still in the machine.

You could hit the machine, but that would hurt your hand.

You could try pushing the buttons again, but the people behind you are getting restless. The distance between you is down to three paces.

Your only hope is to enlist the people behind you as allies

against the machine. You do this by creating a fear that the machine is out of control, that it has turned against you and could turn against them. Here's how that works:

After pounding unsuccessfully on the keys, step back from the machine and turn to those behind you. Calmly, but with a slight edge in your voice, say: "A virus. Oh my God." Slowly shake your head and continue: "I think a virus has got into the machine. I've got to tell them." Then you walk rapidly, not running, into the bank, where you quietly inform a steely-eyed person that you can't figure out how the machine works. Computer viruses are so well-known and fear of them is so widespread that the crowd will have dispersed by the time you get back to the machine, with the steely-eyed person there to help you.

How To Bank on Hallowe'en

The bank this day is all in black and orange. Even the red convertible parked by the customer service counter is orange. Some of the tellers are wearing baseball uniforms. One is dressed like Captain Hook. Another is in a Peter Pan costume. The chief loans officer is Darth Vader. The manager seems to be a Mountie. Or perhaps it *is* a Mountie.

All you want is to withdraw $75.

You approach the wicket, with your usual story about needing more cream for the coffee with which you are washing down an orange-and-black cookie and while you're here you'll just withdraw $75. You say, "Good morning." The teller says "Arrrrrrrrr, matey!!" You hand over your withdrawal slip. The teller removes his eyepatch and squints at it. You hear heavy breathing to one side and see the loans officer bearing down on you, adjusting her helmet. She is going to want to know why you are not taking advantage of the low interest rates on Go-to-the-Caribbean-and-Drink-Stuff-with-Umbrellas-Sticking-out-of-It Loans.

You could run, but you need the $75.

You could say, "Make it snappy, I'm in a hurry," but that wouldn't be you, would it?

Your only hope rests with your own costume, which you have brought with you for just such an emergency. It consists of a Groucho Marx nose and glasses, plus a set of bunny-rabbit ears. Easily concealed in your pocket, the costume can be put on in an instant.

This takes a certain amount of nerve on your part, but not much. It is Hallowe'en, after all. The costume allows you to enter into the spirit of the occasion. At the same time, it renders you less attractive, somehow, as a customer, as a loans prospect. Darth Vader does not want to be seen conducting business with a man, or woman, in a Groucho Marx nose and bunny-rabbit ears. It is beneath Darth's dignity. In all likelihood, the loans officer will merely greet you, wish you happy Hallowe'en, and slip away, breathing heavily and allowing you to leave the bank unscathed to continue with your life.

Chapter 10

At the Church: Is the new religion up to the new religionist?

The New Chuch

Ten Tips for Re-entering the Church

A Clergyperson's Guide to the New Churchgoer

People have been trying to get religion at the same time that religions have been trying to get people. You'd think it would be a natural match, but there have been difficulties and more are ahead.

As it should, an air of mystery surrounds most religious matters, but as best it can be figured out, this is what has been happening: people have been trying to get back to church, and when they get back to church they find it is not as they remembered it. So, another institution has let them down. They lose faith in the faith.

Why did they want to go back in the first place? They outgrew their childhoods, their simple faith, their superstition. Nobody was making them go to church any more. They got some education and discovered some pretty sophisticated secular truths, which helped them through the years ahead, particularly when snappy conversation was required. All of a sudden, grown up and with families of their own, they decide they want to go back.

It may be nostalgia, remembering the sounds and smells and, since nostalgia is selective, forgetting how *long* a church service could take. Or it may be superstition, combined with the first stirrings of mortality: "You may not be there, God, but I've got these chest pains and, in case you are there, long time no see."

It could be good old guilt, a rediscovered reflex, brought on by booze or money or a look at starvation on television coupled with a personal inventory of expensive possessions. A visit to church might show the way out of this decadence. Or it might say it was okay and stop worrying about it.

It may be a desperate attempt to put children on the right path that sends the new churchgoer back – the hope that religious teachings may persuade them, where their parents couldn't, not to smoke, drink, stay out late, and flunk Family Studies.

Or it may be something else entirely with the children – their being caught setting out on a mislaunched voyage of religious discovery. This usually takes place on a Sunday morning when a parent, for whatever reason, has forgotten to sleep in and hears odd noises emanating from the television set.

Parent: "What are you watching?"

Child: "This is neat! A woman was limping up to the stage with crutches and this man hit her on the head and she fell back and when she got up she didn't need crutches any more."

Parent: "Oh, I see. And then what happened?"

Child: "Then the man started asking everyone for money. So I switched over to the one where the man was apologizing and crying."

Parent: "I have a great idea for a little family expedition next Sunday."

The New Church

What do these people think they will find when they re-enter the church? Well, a slightly musty smell in a dark room, just enough light to illuminate the stained glass, the sound of a mighty – although a bit wheezy – organ, lengthy silences, poetic, although sometimes confusing, scriptural passages, and the fear-inspiring yet oddly soothing words of the preacher, encouraging the congregation to fight the good fight, to avoid sin and be forgiven. That would be good.

The church, however, has long since realized that there was no percentage in being like that. Decades of dark carpets, wheezy organs, stained glass, and earnest sermons – what did it get the church but empty pews? So the church decided it had better change, move with society, make the institution a bit more . . . viable.

Specifically, what did that mean? It meant brightening the place up. It meant fewer silences. It meant shake hands with the person behind you and then the person in front of you. It meant toning down the language, making it a bit less violent, a lot less male, quite a bit less poetic, although easier to understand. Most important, it meant guitars.

People played guitars in the church. Strapped them right on and sang to the congregation. Imagine your shock upon re-entering the church, an oddly bright place with waxed floors, to find it full of people playing guitars, electric ones even. The minister himself might be playing a guitar, wearing civilian clothes, without even a tie.

The minister's name is Bob. Everybody calls him that. Nobody calls him Father or Doctor or Reverend. And when he speaks of God, he speaks not of a vengeful God, or an angry one, or even a jealous one. He speaks of a caring God, a nurturing, synergistic one. A supportive God.

This is not what you came all the way back to the church to find. But, on the other hand, if you wanted things to stay the way they were, why did you leave in the first place?

Here you are, then, and you have to learn how to church all over again.

Ten Tips for Re-entering the Church

1. Remember, just because you are in a church does not mean you are on television. Not all church services are televised. So waving is not necessary. Neither is makeup.

2. Neither is the public confession of sin. Standing up and tearfully revealing your sins is inappropriate. Nowadays most people go to church to forget about sin.

3. Even the private confession of sin is not always welcomed. The minister doesn't think he needs to know, upon first meeting you, everything that you have done wrong in the past ten years, or even the past ten hours.

4. The minister wouldn't mind some investment advice, however.

5. Not all of your co-parishioners share your feeling for the good old church. Loud whispers of "This should be slower" in the middle of hymns will not be appreciated.

6. The collection plate does not take MasterCard in all dioceses.

7. Let the new language go by. You may not like to hear phrases such as "Let not him or her that girdeth on his or her harness boast him or herself as he or she that putteth it off." But the new words will either last or not last regardless of what you think. There is no use in continually leaping to your feet, brandishing your King James Version and crying out, "That's not what it says here."

8. If your kids are used to television and not used to church services, remind them that it is not permissible to get up and get a snack in the middle.

9. Remind them also that there is no such thing as "half-time."

10. Generally speaking, video cameras are allowed only at weddings and funerals.

The difficulty of adjustment works both ways. The churches, too, won't find it easy to accommodate the thousands of nostalgia buffs who pour in all of a sudden for doses of that old-time religion. The churches will have to "know thine enemy," as someone put it, or "check out the house," as someone else put it more charitably. For the benefit of organized religion, then, the following is presented.

A Clergyperson's Guide to the New Churchgoer

1. The new churchgoer likes the old phraseology, particularly its emphasis on weapons and battle. Though the new liturgy prohibits violent imagery, it would be a nice gesture to leave a sword or two in some of the biblical stories, and try to make a bit clearer the new line about "beating their plowshares into plowshares." It would also be good to allow David his five smooth stones, instead of the "five injunctions" that are now in the scripture.

2. Word of mouth can cause church attendance to swell, and one way of getting favourable word of mouth is ample parking.

3. Do not, after the service, ask the new churchgoer about his golf game. Do ask him for investment advice.

4. When children of the new churchgoers hear some of the exciting Bible stories, they will want to know if those stories are out on video games.

5. The new churchgoer is an audio buff and will want to offer you helpful suggestions about the acoustics of the church. These can be tolerated. The suggestion that the organ be converted to digital is about where the line should be drawn.

6. The new churchgoer may feign a purist's shock over the church-owned high-rise looming at the back of the property, but he loves to talk real estate, especially as an alternative to talking about the Old Testament.

7. While denunciation of sin from the pulpit can titillate the congregation and cause favourable word of mouth, it is better to make such denunciations general. Condemning

worldly pleasures of the flesh is acceptable; condemning tax avoidance is not.

8. That notwithstanding, a lot of new churchgoers will want to discuss sins, but theirs are penny-ante stuff. If you are the minister, pretend that you are interested, and even express shock at times. The parishioner wants to feel he got his or her money's worth.

Parishioner: "I could have paid the parking ticket, Father–"

Minister: "Call me Bob."

Parishioner: "I could have paid the parking ticket, Bob, but I didn't –"

Minister: "Oh, no."

Parishioner: "And you know what I did next?"

Minister: "Don't tell me unless you are absolutely comfortable with this."

Parishioner: "I feel that I can trust you, Father –"

Minister: "Bob."

Parishioner: "Bob. Then I parked in a 'No Stopping' area."

Minister: "You didn't!"

Parishioner: "I did. I was late for my weight-loss clinic."

Minister: "It must be difficult for you to talk about this."

Parishioner: "Yes, but I feel better for having told you."

Minister: "You are forgiven. Go and thin no more."

Chapter 11

Government: Enough to worry about without you

Over the years modern democratic government has reached such a high degree of sophistication that it no longer needs people to govern. It can function at full capacity with no reference at all to the outside world. The modern democratic politician, meanwhile, has reached a level at which it is no longer necessary to have ideas or take positions. This means that the modern democratic voter can, if he or she chooses, just sit back and watch. For the most part that is what the modern democratic voter does – although some modern democratic voters choose to sit back and not watch, and some modern democratic watchers choose to sit back and not vote.

We have to work with government and politicians, encourage them to give it their best, otherwise our system fails and we wind up with a different one, just as inefficient and far less amusing. There is more to being a citizen than simply watching the TV news and turning out to vote every time somebody is running for something. We also have to interact with politicians and bureaucrats, to make sure they don't forget that we're out there. With every passing year, this becomes more difficult.

A Closed System

Government now governs itself. It may not be exactly what the founding fathers and mothers had in mind when they thought up the idea of self-government, but there it is. The government governs itself and the people are off to one side, wondering what to do. A look at the modern democratic government shows it humming along, very busy looking after its own needs. For a start, people have to be paid, the pay cheques have to be made out, put in envelopes, addressed, distributed. The people who handle the envelopes have to eat lunch and have coffee, so there has to be a cafeteria, where there have to be people working.

Since all those people are there, addressing envelopes and working in the cafeteria, they need to have a place to park, and the parking lot needs attendants, who in turn need supervisors. Such people are at the heart of modern democratic government.

With so many people required to address envelopes and work in the cafeteria and the parking lot, administrators are needed to make sure everything goes all right and the workers are being productive. The administrators need support staff, secretaries and people to answer the telephone and say the administrators are in a meeting. The administrators cannot be in a meeting without people to be in a meeting with, so some people like that are necessary too. All of them need secretaries.

The secretaries need computers. Computers are always breaking down or behaving weirdly, so it is necessary to hire other people to fix the computers when they break down, as well as to perform the vital function of telling the secretaries that it is not the computer's fault when it doesn't work. Other people are needed to make sure the elevators run, the faxes have enough paper, and the telephones are not being misused. In order to ensure the latter, it is necessary to hire people to instruct other workers on the way the phone system works.

Not a single one of these people needs to have any contact with people outside the world of government. Administrators administer, cooks cook, typists type, computer fixers fix – all of these people have a full day's work to do without anybody in the outside world making a single request.

It works the same way for politicians, at least between elections. They stand up in the council chambers and legislatures and make speeches that are in response to speeches that someone else made the day before, sparked by a real or imagined insult to their integrity, to which someone else raised a point of order, which is being debated now. The matter may be referred to a committee. The committee will need staff.

So that is an important secret of modern democratic government, at all levels – local, provincial, national. *It can keep itself completely occupied just looking after its own needs.* It does not take much imagination, then, to recognize how inconvenient it is for modern democratic government when someone shows up from outside wanting the government to do something. The system was not designed to handle such people. The system was designed to keep the system going.

Breaking into the System

This makes it difficult for you when you have to enter the world of government for help with a problem. Perhaps a relative overseas needs a visa to come and live with you. Perhaps a neighbour wants to build an addition that will take away all your sun. Perhaps you want to expand your business and need to know how much you are allowed to pollute. In each case, you will enter the world of government, and the world of government will not thank you for it.

No time has been set aside for you in the day's busy schedule. The typists have to type memos about previous memos;

the administrators have to read memos about previous meetings and prepare for new meetings about the new memos; the computer is down and the situation to which you refer cannot be located in the files. This is no wonder: what you are bringing is new work. If modern democratic government is to deal with you, it will have to do work that it has not been doing. And it already has enough to do. The day is structured in such a way that there is just enough time to do everything that needs to be done, provided you don't show up.

But show up you do, with your request. Be ready for one of the following responses:

1. "We don't handle that here."

2. "The person who handles that is on vacation."

3. "Have you brought in a completed J-274B form?"

4. "The person who handles that is in Chicoutimi learning French."

5. "Fill this out and come back in three weeks."

6. "Take this down the hall, get someone to sign it, go up to the third floor and have your picture taken, then come back here next Tuesday."

7. "The person who handles that is dead."

8. "You'll need your father's birth certificate, your mother's marriage certificate, and three pieces of identification plus a notarized J-274C form."

Each of these statements means that no one here wants to have anything to do with your problem. Somehow you must get their attention. How to do it?

The Reporter Gambit

Many people make the mistake of pretending to be reporters, thinking that will get the government moving. It never works. The government has a well-established procedure it swings into whenever it learns that a reporter is on the premises.

You: "I'd like to talk to your supervisor. I'm a reporter."

Government: "I'm sorry, I'm not authorized to speak to reporters. You will have to deal with our Public Information Section."

You: "Where is the Public Information Section?"

Government: "I'm sorry, I'm not authorized to say that."

Reporters are shunted around even more than ordinary people. It should be a tip-off to you that reporters, when they want to get the inside story, always masquerade as ordinary people. They know that pretending to be a reporter doesn't work.

There is a school of thought that pretending *not* to be a reporter is a better strategy. And it is true that pretending not to be a reporter will immediately cause government to suspect that you are a reporter. But then government will say, "So what?" and begin implementing the well-established procedure.

What does work, however, is pretending to *know* a reporter. Government is afraid of reporters. Reporters might report something. That is why the well-established procedures have been established. But the well-established procedures are time-consuming and distracting and the government would just as soon not have to go into them. So invoking the *threat* of a reporter showing up is more effective than being a reporter.

You: "I need to see someone about a visa for my uncle."

Government: "I'm sorry, the person responsible for that is dead."

You: "Dead, eh? That would interest my friends at the *News-Press*."

Government: "Perhaps she isn't dead. Let me check. Helen, is Ms Stanhope still dead? Oh, she's not? OK. I'm sorry, my mistake. Happens all the time. Ms Stanhope will see you soon. In the meantime, please enjoy a complimentary balloon."

The Politician Ploy

Pretending to be a politician runs similar risks. Well-established procedures exist here too. If an elected politician turns up, most of the government simply walks away. Some of it hides in the photocopy room, some of it goes out for an early lunch. It is understood by everyone in government that as soon as an elected politician asks a question, someone will have to prepare an answer, and that will cause a chain reaction of work. The answer will have to be edited, circulated, translated, revised, the revisions retyped, rediscussed, recirculated, and released. Much necessary internal work will have to be delayed, including the much-discussed Draft Policy on Draft Policies, if a politician is allowed into the loop. That is why everyone vanishes so quickly when you attempt your politician impersonation.

On the other hand, the threat of political intervention has power. The government does not want politicians to appear. The government does not want to have to disappear. Every time the government disappears, it gets farther and farther behind in its work.

You: "My father, the well-known senator, asked me to see if you could help out on a visa matter."

Government: "Would the senator be coming to see us personally?"

You: "Not necessarily."

Government: "We'll be glad to help. What is your favourite colour balloon?"

Threatening Suicide

Don't even think about it.

You: "If I can't see someone right now about my uncle's visa, I'm going to kill myself."

Government: "I'm sorry, that's not allowed here."

Chapter 12

In the Hospital: What to do till the doctor leaves

How To Recognize a Doctor in the Hospital

How To Be a Patient

Just Visiting

How To Be the Best Hospital Visitor Ever

SPOT THE DOC QUIZ

A. CHIEF NUTRITIONIST

B. CRANIAL SURGEON

C. TV ACTOR

A. PHYSIOTHERAPIST

B. FLOWER DELIVERER

C. HEAD OF OBSTETRICS

A. VISITOR

B. VOLUNTEER

C. PROSTATE SURGEON

A. HEART SURGEON

B. NURSE

C. TV ACTOR

You could always tell who the doctors were in the hospital of days gone by. The doctor was a man. He wore a suit under his white lab coat. The lab coat had a stethoscope sticking out of it. Women opened doors for him and walked a few steps behind. Those were nurses. Nurses were always women and wore starchy white hats that sat on top of their hair.

It was rather uncomplicated being around a hospital in those days. You knew who the doctors and the nurses were. Everybody else just worked there. If you were a patient waking up, you knew instantly you were in a hospital because everything smelled like ether. Even the flowers smelled like ether. If a woman in white came to see you, it was a nurse. If a man in white came to see you, it was a doctor.

Was everything better in those days? Not exactly. The nurses didn't like opening the doors for the doctors; and they didn't much like the fact that all the doctors were men. Not all the patients did either. The doctors probably liked everything fine although nobody liked the smell of ether all that much. But at least everybody knew what was going on: when you said: "How is she, Doc?" the doc didn't say, "I'm afraid I can't help you. I'm the associate nutritionist."

That is what goes on now. Everybody in the hospital is confused – at least the patients and the visitors are. The place brims over with nurses, nurses' aides, volunteers of one type or another, nutritionists, social workers, administrators, occupational therapists, recreational therapists, physical therapists, and whatnot. They all seem to wear uniforms. None of the uniforms is distinguishable to a civilian. A patient who asks for a glass of water runs the risk of offending an eminent surgeon, or else being turned down by someone who does not have the authority to issue a glass of water.

How To Recognize a Doctor in the Hospital

There is no particular reason why you should want a doctor right now. A doctor has many patients and there is a time set aside for the doctor to be interested in you (if you are a patient) or your loved one (if you are a visitor). If you locate a doctor at a time which is not the time set aside, the doctor will look blank. Still, if you insist on knowing which of those many men and women is a doctor, here are some guidelines:

1. Generally speaking, the doctors have the worst shoes in the hospital. Everyone else needs to be neat and well-turned-out to keep their jobs. Doctors don't. Doctors like to give the impression that they are too busy and have to run too fast to give any time to what they wear or how they look. Often this is true. Surgeons like to look as if they just took a minute off from a particularly gory operation. They don't mind having little bits of blood on their clothing. And neither should you, as long as it's not yours.

In summary, that man or woman with the Hush Puppies under the stained lab coat – that's the doc.

2. If you see someone spending a lot of time with a patient, soothing and solicitous – that's a lawyer.

3. Doctors are very busy, and if they stopped to chat with patients, they would not have time to stop and chat with other patients, which they don't have time for anyway. If you are in a hospital room and a person with bad shoes strolls into the room, inquires after your health, nods, grunts, and leaves quickly – that's the doc. If he leaves without coming to a complete stop, that's the surgeon.

4. Unlike nurses, doctors prefer not to use the English language in speaking to non-medical people. It took them many years of study to learn the language they speak with each other, and they are not going to depart from it in speaking to you. Like politicians, doctors are a bit afraid of having people understand what they say. This may have something to do with the escalation of damages in malpractice suits that they hear about on television. Or it may just be that they like to have secrets. Whereas a nurse will tell you that your broken leg is healing slowly, the doctor will say there is a degree of reticence in the area of trauma in the tibia. Or so it sounds to you.

5. It goes without saying that doctors understand foreign languages such as that spoken over hospital address systems. When the public address system says, "Dr. Casey, neezer scrimble on eight," and you see a woman with bad shoes walk swiftly down the hall – that's Doc Casey.

6. Doctors are very patient with patients, but a bit vague. If you ask, "Does that mean my leg isn't healing as fast as it should?" they'll smile and say, "Not exactly, but something like that."

7. Doctors don't refer to patients as "we" any more. If someone walks up to your bed and says, "How did we sleep last night? Are we feeling any better?" – that's not the doc. It may be an administrator. Administrators often worry about patients being unhappy, because administrators know that patients are capable of making, or refusing to make, bequests.

8. However, doctors don't refer to patients by their first names either. Everybody else in the hospital does that. Everybody else in the hospital can walk into your room and call you by your first name, even though you don't know theirs – either because you were never formally introduced, or because you were heavily sedated at the time introductions took place. The doctor calls you Mr. or Mrs. or Miss. So that's a sign. A man or woman walks quickly into your room and doesn't call you by your first name – that's the doc.

How To Be a Patient

You probably want attention, because you don't feel so hot, otherwise you wouldn't be in the hospital in the first place. The obvious thing to do, the thing the novice patient does, is ring the buzzer and ask to see a doctor. But it is wrong. There probably isn't a doctor within miles of the place. Hospitals don't like to admit that; patients assume that a hospital has doctors in it. To a patient, having doctors in it is one of the defining characteristics of a hospital. It would be shattering if, when you asked to see a doctor, the person you asked said: "I'd love to help you, but we haven't the foggiest idea where any of the doctors are. I'm sure one will turn up eventually."

The mythology of doctors, built up in years of medical dramas in the movies and on television, is that doctors spend all their time racing from one potentially fatal situation to another and never stop for lunch. But this is not true. Calling for a doctor will just get you a reputation as a crybaby, and when you really want the doctor, such as when a black widow spider creeps into your room and bites you, no one will believe you. Crying doctor is very much like crying wolf, although it is much easier to recognize a wolf when it comes into your room.

1. The doctor will come when it is time for the doctor to

come. You cannot affect the process. If you must see someone, ring your buzzer and someone will come. Pretend it is a
doctor and tell the person what is bothering you. The person
will bring you a glass of water. Be grateful for the water. If the
person who comes to see you is a doctor, the person will ask
someone else to bring you a glass of water.

2. If you are really old, you can get away with asking
people who they are. Otherwise, there is no point. There
are people in white uniforms, blue uniforms, pink uniforms, yellow uniforms, and they all act as if they know
what they are doing. If they wanted you to know who they
are, they would tell you. As long as they bring you water
and pills and take away your dirty dishes, what does it really
matter? You could demand to know who they are, but that
would brand you as a troublemaker. The important thing is
that *they* know who they are.

3. Faking an injury is a great way of getting attention
almost everywhere. You fall to the ground clutching your
ankle. But it is a pretty dumb thing to try in a hospital. For
one thing, you have to get out of bed to fall to the ground
and clutch your ankle. What if they don't let you out of
bed?

Secondly, why pretend there is something wrong with
you? If there wasn't something wrong with you, you
wouldn't be there. If you convince the hospital that there is
something *else* wrong with you, they will simply move you to
another ward, where you will have to learn who everybody is
all over again. In the new ward they will assume that you
already got a glass of water in the old ward, so it will be hours
before anybody brings you anything.

4. The most difficult information to get in a hospital is
when you can leave. Hospitals don't like to say, until five
minutes before. Then someone will come into your room
and ask: "Is anyone coming to get you?" The secrecy on this
matter is not easy to figure out. The hospital may be afraid

that, given any warning at all, you will pack up all the towels and glasses and some of the better-looking prints from the wall.

A useful technique is to ask every uniformed person who comes into your room how long you can stay. If the hospital gets the idea that you are really enjoying yourself, it will let you know very quickly when you will be let out.

5. As we have seen, visitors can be useful, so they should be treated well. Pretend you are glad to see them. Your visitor had to come all the way here, line up to get into the parking garage, and buy the flowers. The least you can do is pretend to be happy you have a visitor and pretend that you have never, ever, seen flowers before. Ask for news of the outside world. It won't interest you at all – at least, not as much as your symptoms – but your visitor is not as interested in your symptoms as you are, not even in your discussion of how they have changed since the last time your visitor was there. Then pretend to be very tired, which allows the visitor to leave with a clear conscience and you to get back to your glass of water.

6. The thing hospital patients fear most is being lost by the system. The movies are full of that. A patient gets lost, lies unnoticed in a hospital for months, and then suddenly has a facelift when what was really wrong was appendicitis. To avoid being lost, it is important to become memorable. But you must be memorable in a positive way, not just as the crybaby in A408 who keeps whining about black widow spiders. The hospital will *want* to lose you if you behave like that. A better way to be memorable is to be cheerful. Extremely cheerful. Hardly anyone is cheerful in a hospital, except for the people who sell flowers and the man who cleans out the goldfish tank. Patients are not known for their cheerfulness. But if you tie balloons to your bed, play practical jokes on the staff, offer candies to the nurses, and sing Christmas carols no matter what the season, it is likely

that the hospital will know who you are and not give you a facelift by mistake.

7. If worried about getting lost in the hospital system, remember that someone knows who you are and someone knows what the hospital's plans for you are. But remember also the Law of Hospitals, which is as follows: The person who knows about your case is never the person you are talking to.

Just Visiting

It takes co-operation to make a great hospital. And that co-operation has to come from all sorts of people. The doctors, the nurses, the patients, the administrators, the support staff – they all need each other. The importance of the visitor, however, has frequently been overlooked. Yet the visitor's impact on the system is enormous. Much of the hospital economy – the flower and gift shoppes, the parking garage, the coffee machine, the newspaper-vending box – would disappear without the visitor. Yet no one thanks the visitor. The only time any attention is paid to the visitor is when a nurse asks him to go stand in the hall for fifteen minutes while some embarrassing procedure is performed. This callousness, this neglect, makes the visitor's task difficult. But accomplished hospital visitors are not daunted. The challenge is to be the best they can be, and at the very least, not too bad.

How To Be the Best Hospital Visitor Ever

1. Allow yourself time to learn the layout of the shopping concourse. The best hospitals have them, a veritable soukh of little boutiques in which it is possible to get lost easily and be late for your visit. Realizing how late you are, you will panic and buy something totally inappropriate as a gift. When you show up forty-five minutes late with a giant fuzzy turtle, your grandmother is not going to be grateful and you are going to be out fifty bucks.

2. The patient does not want to be pitied too much. Tell him he must feel terrible and he will. Ask him to describe all the things wrong with him and he will, thus becoming even more conscious of them. (The hard-hearted visitor who merely wants to be excused early will use this tactic, causing the patient so much discomfort that he will ring for the doctor, causing someone to come with a glass of water and allowing the visitor to slip away.)

3. At the same time, the patient does not want to be told that everything is absolutely fine. Here is an example of the wrong approach:

"So, you look great and I understand you're all better. Isn't that wonderful?"

For one thing, the patient wouldn't be there if she was all better. And if she does in fact feel fine, she wants a chance to enjoy that feeling by contrasting it with how lousy she felt a few days ago. She has earned feeling fine. If you keep telling her nothing is wrong, she will start to feel guilty for taking up a hospital bed. What you should say is:

"You look a lot better. I bet you're looking forward to being 100 per cent again."

4. The patient needs a chance to talk about his operation. Nothing else in life is so interesting. It is far more interesting than the world situation. Your job is to be interested. Some day you will have an operation and will want to talk.

If you change the subject, you must be delicate about it. You can't say: "Speaking of shoulders, I see where they're widening Highway 7." More subtlety than that is called for. Stick to a subject the patient cares about. Better to say: "How's the water around here?"

5. If the room is dark or overheated – both of which are likely – it is not your duty to point that out. You will only be there half an hour, and after you leave the patient is going to have to live with a dark and overheated room. Better for you to point out how nice and comfortable it is, how good the

flowers look, how great the view is if you just look around the corner a bit, and how the sealed windows make it impossible for black widow spiders to come in.

6. Your views on cutbacks in health-care spending, while undoubtedly relevant and interesting, might be appropriately expressed at a time other than when the meat loaf has just appeared.

Chapter 13

At School: Why Johnny can't sleep

How Not To Be Afraid in School

How To Be Cool Without Being a Total Idiot

How To Get Through School
Without Killing Your Kids

How To Meet the School Board

It's time we had a hard look at our educational system and decided to stop having hard looks at it. All those hard looks are making it hard for the system to operate. The teachers are frustrated, the parents are suspicious, the government is taking back all the money, and the children are scared silly.

None of this happened before people started taking hard looks at the educational system. The year usually credited with starting hard looks at the educational system is 1957, the year the Soviet Union launched the Sputnik, gaining a lead in technology they would never relinquish until the entire nation collapsed and fell apart in 1991. The hard looks that began in 1957 intensified over the years until no one wanted much to go to school in the Eighties and no one wanted to pay for schools in the Nineties. Taxpayers began demanding that schools not spend so much, the schools began to decline owing to underfunding, and the opponents of education spending said: "See, we told you they weren't worth the money." Passenger train service disappeared about the same way.

School used to be a fairly easygoing place unless you got Miss Dewey or someone who scared you into working hard in math. Mostly, you got good grades or you didn't, hung around the gym a bit, worried primarily about the dances, thought about university if you had the grades and the money, thought about something else if you didn't, such as getting a job, which wasn't a problem. There was a bit of drinking in the upper grades, but no one had heard of drugs or *AIDS* or computer literacy or French immersion. And smoking was harmless and very cool. You could start doing it as soon as you were old enough to see over the counter to buy a deck of weeds.

Now look at it. The first thing five-year-olds learn when they arrive at school is that they should have been there when they were four-year-olds because everybody else was. Then they learn that they should never trust anybody who talks to them on the street. They worry about that.

By the time they get out of junior high school, they are also worried about booze, drugs, and *AIDS*. They are told not to share needles. When they get into high school they are told that they had better master computers or else they will have no future at all. Girls are told that they are letting their entire gender down if they don't excel at maths and science. Boys are told to have designated drivers. They worry that their Grade 9 marks will keep them out of university and deprive them forever of a good life.

They are told that much is at stake. And perhaps it is. Whether it is or not, school has become solemn. There is no reason it has to be.

How Not To Be Afraid in School

1. Those kids you think are so cool – they're just as scared as you are. They just laugh loud. The louder they laugh, the scareder they are.

2. The teacher is a human being, an actual person. After

school he goes home and has to mow the lawn. He gets toothaches and his car doesn't always start.

3. By this time next month, the teacher will have stopped thinking about how you flunked this test.

4. You are not the only person in Grade 10 who hasn't done it. Hardly anyone has done it, and at least some of those who have didn't enjoy it at all.

5. Everyone is *not* looking at you. Everyone does *not* see how funny your hair looks. Mostly everyone is worried about how their own hair looks.

6. The song you made the mistake of saying you hated, the one everybody else thinks is so great, will be gone in two weeks.

7. You are not the only person in Grade 12 who hasn't done it.

8. Half the people who said they were drunk last Saturday night weren't. Half the ones who were are ashamed of themselves.

9. Most of the successful people in the world didn't know what they wanted to be when they were your age.

10. Many of the most successful people in the world are still no good at math.

Much of the anxiety felt by students has nothing to do with course work or the possibility of not making the track team. It has to do with being cool, something that is not easy. Somewhere out there, or Up There, is someone who decides what is cool this week, and not next week, but no one knows who that is and therefore it is impossible to find out whether it is absolutely necessary to buy this year's skateboard or this week's colour in basketball shoes. They may be gone next week. They may be absolutely essential as far down the road as next September. Somebody knows, but nobody is telling. Failing that, how is a kid to know what is cool, and how to get around it if what is cool is also dumb?

How To Be Cool Without Being a Total Idiot

1. You feel like a loser, right, when you get in the car and you want to drive off like a cool guy, but first you have to fasten your seat-belt and do the shoulder check. You can't not do it because all that stuff from Driver Training is too deeply ingrained. Also you don't want to get hurt. Mostly, you don't want your folks to take the car away. The back seat is full of cool kids and this is a test.

    a. Take refuge in irony. "Shoulder check!" you announce loudly, as you do the shoulder check. The kids will laugh and understand. They went to Driver Training too.

    b. Tell them about the movie you rented the other night where Sean Penn, Steve McQueen, Gary Cooper, Lauren Bacall, Tom Cruise, Kevin Costner, Madonna, Kiefer Sutherland, Kathleen Turner, Eddie Murphy, or Abbott and Costello did a shoulder check.

2. You are at a party and you throw up because you are drunk. Say it is because you were mixing your drinks. Kids believe that stuff.

3. You are at a party and you are sober. Resist the temptation to apologize for your behaviour. Say you are not drinking because:

    a. You are giving your liver a rest. Fourteen-year-olds will think that is romantic.

    b. You don't need it.

    c. You are driving.

    d. Sex is better when you are totally aware of all your nerve endings.

    e. You don't need it any more. Some teen-agers are into co-dependency already and will dig that.

    f. You are only ten and don't want to start for a couple more years.

4. You can get away with almost anything if you are willing to be a rebel. The rebel is a respected figure in all schools.

But there is a fine line between being a rebel and being a geek, and not all people recognize it. When you are being a rebel, you may have to announce it. A good time is when you suddenly realize that you are wearing your hat backwards when everybody else is wearing theirs frontwards. If you are doing it because you are a rebel, that is cool.

5. Being a rebel, you will fall in with other rebels, not all of whom you may want to have fallen in with. The rebels may be into drugs, for example, or skateboards. Wanting to avoid such behaviour puts you in a difficult position. Can you rebel against being a rebel? Isn't that the same thing as being a conformist? It is a tough call, but no one said there weren't tough calls in life. This may be a time when you simply have to turn your hat around and march out the door.

6. Being cool means being wise to the media. If you can get on television, explaining What It Means To Be a Kid Today, you will be a hero among your peers. The media always want to know what it means to be a kid today, partly because editors have kids and want to know what they are up to without having to ask them directly, and because reporters want to know if they are still young enough to understand kids. The key to getting on the news is to present something scary enough to shock the viewer, yet familiar enough to convince the viewer that Kids Will Always Be Kids.

a. The media know all about sex, drugs, and booze. They are the traditional horror stories. Sex-crazed kids using drugs and booze. Or drug-crazed kids using sex. Or whatever. That won't shock them, unless you can produce a new kind of drug that no one grown up has ever used. You can also shock them by saying that kids are *not* using drugs and booze. Or that you know for a fact that many high school kids (or even elementary school kids) are virgins.

b. Witchcraft and devil worship are always of interest.

Weird computer games played late at night have a fasci-
nation for the media as well.

c. Depression is good, widespread suicide still a winner.

d. Hatred of parents will always make air. If you really
want to shock parents, make sure you say that what you
hate parents for is their materialism, the fact that they
give you all these *things* and think it will substitute for
love.

e. Some television stations are better equipped tech-
nically than others. The ones with state-of-the-art technology can bleep out your swear-words, put an electronic mask in front of your face and a moving bar over
the dirty words on your T-shirt. If they have the technology to do that, they love to use it. But make sure to
ask first. Swearing and wearing a T-shirt with dirty
words on it might just keep you off the air.

Much of the anxiety felt by students is passed on to them
by their parents, who are full of anxiety themselves. A lot of
that they get from the media. Reading newspapers and
watching the television news, they discover, each day, some
new horrible fact about the educational system – how it ranks
below that of Tibet in computer literacy, how our universities complain that high school graduates cannot count to
twenty, how our industries complain that university graduates cannot count to thirty, how cocaine runs out of the high
school water fountain, how gangs armed with atomic weapons patrol the hallways.

The parents assume that whatever is going wrong is their
kids' fault, although in their heart of hearts they suspect it is
their own. If only they hadn't demanded all those tax cuts. If
only they had spent less time with clients and more time getting involved in the school.

How To Get Through School
Without Killing Your Kids

1. Education is important, yes, but this particular C- on this particular quiz in this particular week in Grade 3 is not important, not in the greater scheme of things. Try not to make it a Lesson in Life for your kid. Try not to let it get you started on where you went wrong. You didn't go wrong; the kid messed up the test. Probably she was having fun doing something that will be far more important to her later in life, like riding a bicycle.

2. If three kids in the neighbourhood, including your own, don't make the basketball team, that is no reason to pool your resources and hire a lawyer.

3. On Meet the Teacher night, resist the temptation to corner the teacher for a private chat about the things that make your kid special. Instead, give the teacher a nice surprise by asking about the course content instead of the marking scheme.

4. The person who told you that playing computer games increases your kid's computer skills was just trying to sell computers. In the Game of Life, a joystick is never used. If you bought a computer anyway, try to be helpful by not demonstrating your skills at shooting down enemy space-ships just when the kid has to type an essay.

5. If you have strong ideas about the school's role in promoting progressive attitudes, patriotism, and/or prayer, try to keep them to yourself.

6. It is possible that things have changed since you went to school. It is possible that your kids do not need to know how things were when you went to school, particularly the part about how you knew how to have fun. They know how to have fun – or at least they think they do.

7. Faithful attendance at school concerts, plays, and sports events is praiseworthy. Your post-game or post-concert critique of what went wrong is not absolutely necessary.

8. If you can't be a faithful attender of school concerts, plays, and sports events, make sure you don't give the impression it is because you have more important things to do. A good-luck call from the car phone is not as touching as you might think.

9. There is no logic in the way students dress and there is no point in using logic – such as the proven fact that something looks stupid – in persuading your kids not to do such things as wearing hats backward or having their boxer shorts stick out from below their basketball shorts. A child above a certain age – seven, say – will not wear gloves, no matter what. Whatever the style of dress you hate, the important thing to remember is that it will change, and not because of anything you do or say.

10. The biggest enemies of your peace of mind – and therefore your child's – are your fellow parents. They will fill you full of stories about their child's accomplishments, their child's chances of getting into the best university, the prizes the child has won, the goals scored, the flattering things the teacher said. Just remember that parents are like that. They will grow out of it.

How To Meet the School Board

At least once in your life you will have to go to the school board. There will be a dispute that cannot be resolved by ordinary people and it will be necessary to take it to the top. When you arrive at the top, extinguish all smoking materials and keep certain things in mind.

1. School-board logic is not the same as ordinary-people logic. Here is an example of school-board logic, drawn from real life:

The school board closes a high school down because of declining enrolment. The declining enrolment is in another school, but that school's enrolment will be brought up to specifications if this school is closed. After a few years, the population increases and it is decided to reopen the school, but not as a high school, as a junior high school. In order to do this, another junior high school, which had been threatened with demolition, and which parents had lobbied to save, will be converted to an elementary school. First, however, it will be torn down, then rebuilt.

Such things go on every week at school boards around the world and the newspapers duly report them as if they were part of reality.

2. If you understand this logic, you should probably be a trustee, rather than a mere parent. If you do not understand the logic, you should understand how the decision is arrived at. The board has experts who work for it. The experts are in touch with experts from all around the world. They have the latest statistics, the latest financial projections, the latest demographics, the latest educational theories. If all that was available to you, you'd make a lot of stupid mistakes too.

3. Faced with such overpowering resources, the poor neighbourhood parents' group has few means at its disposal, although some tried-and-tested methods are available. A collective holding of the breath until you turn blue can have great media impact.

4. Once you have the media's attention, you will need to back it up with statistics. Reporters need statistics so that their editors can have graphics made illustrating the statistics. If you do not provide your own statistics, the reporters will get some from somewhere else. Is it ethical for you to invent statistics? Not really. But if the statistics you invent are going to be misinterpreted anyway, the harm in inventing them is considerably diminished. Anyway, even truthful statistics can be effective if used correctly. Here are some good statistics that can be put to just about any purpose you want:

a. xx per cent of the students in our neighbourhood are concerned about the future.

b. Vehicular traffic has risen xx per cent in the last xx years.

c. The dropout rate has increased xx per cent.

d. Nutritionists report a decline of xx per cent in the nutritional intake of the average student.

e. xx per cent of mothers now work outside the home.

Taken by themselves, none of those numbers means anything, but put together, assembled into a colour graph in the newspaper, they can make a telling case for keeping the old school open, tearing it down, changing it to an elementary school, changing it to a vocational school, adding school bus routes, increasing the budget for school lunches – just about anything you can name.

5. Be aware that the board will counter with its own statistics. However, because they are drawn up by experts from out of town, no one will understand them and the media will not be able to put them into colour graphs.

6. Sometimes the only way to have any influence with the school board is to get your friends to become trustees, or even to become one yourself. If you are contemplating this, be aware that the modern voter is sophisticated and discerning. Confronted with a confusing array of choices for school board, he will snub all but those whose names come highest on the ballot. Make sure that your friends, before they enter the race, change their names to something that begins with the letter A.

Chapter 14

Today's Tavern: Enough to drive you away from drink

How To Have Fun at a Tavern
Without Actually Saying Anything

How To Have Silent Fun in the New Upscale Tavern

Things People Say in Taverns Which Should Be
Followed Immediately by Your Saying "I Have To Be
Going Now."

Five Reasons You Are Not Drinking

How To Be a Non-Drinker at the Tavern

How To Be Drunk

The modern tavern is considered a big improvement over the old one. It is bright and has windows. It has things to do. You can get up and stroll around, chit-chat with the folks. There is music. There are games. There are plants. There are women and people who are not drunk. There is decor. All in all, it is a more wholesome environment than the tavern used to be.

The old tavern, on the other hand, was a place so hamstrung by regulations that all you could do in it was get drunk, and if you didn't, you had been wasting your time all night. After you got drunk, you got in your great big car and tried to get home, after first stopping for a pizza, you and the whole ball team, and making clever remarks to the waitress.

Now you can go and see your friends and have two light beers and some healthy snacks, or some nachos if you are feeling really decadent, and someone who has not been drinking at all will drive you home, in time for the news.

The tavern caters to families. Husbands and wives can go together. Wives can go without husbands, the atmosphere is so non-threatening. The decor is interesting. There are all these little corners with amusing things hung on the walls and there is always a game of some kind on one of the many TV sets. There are multicoloured drinks. And there are trivia contests and karaoke nights and little electronic poker machines, even basketball hoops to shoot at.

Just as the old tavern did, the modern tavern divides families, but now it is in a new way: Now families get into arguments about which *kind* of tavern they will be going to. Will it be the country music one around the corner, the punk one down the street, the fern bar where all the lawyers go, the sports bar, or what? Major lifestyle choices loom almost every evening.

The tavern has come a long way. Thirty years ago you had a choice of which place with a concrete floor you wanted to drink in. The tables were round things with Formica tops and there was only one TV set, which usually didn't have a game on it anyway, and no music was allowed, except in the fancier places which had a woman who played the organ rather than a piano. This was because having someone play the piano would encourage people to sing. You were stuck at your table. If you wanted to go to another table – although heaven knows why you would – you had to signal for the waiter, who would carry your beer over there for you. That was the rule.

There was no lite beer either, and no foreign stuff and none of the ones from the little local breweries with the little local names. There were no lite snacks; you had a choice between the pickled eggs or the chuckwagon sandwich, which was something like salami with something like cheese, heated up somehow and which you could eat all right if you put a lot of mustard on it.

However, conversation was possible in those days. There was no loud rock music you had to shout over, no electronic games. Because there was no music, people didn't have to shout to be heard and you didn't have to shout to be heard over the other people shouting to be heard. And there weren't people getting up and wandering around all the time to play some game. Your friends pulled up a chair and paid attention to the conversation, particularly the ones who had their backs to the TV set. No one was trying to meet girls because why would you go to a tavern to meet girls. You went to a tavern to drink beer and talk about sports. Sometimes you would talk about beer, sometimes comparative religion, and sometimes, very late at night, you would talk about women or Diefenbaker, but mostly it was about sports.

No one talked about relationships, which had not been invented yet. And no one talked about trivia, although some people remembered more about old TV shows than others did. Trivia had not become part of the economy. The television set was not constantly moving from one game to another, from hockey in Pittsburgh to baseball in Chicago to football in Denver, to a replay of last year's football in Los Angeles, to wrestling, to big trucks crushing small trucks, to women in bikinis playing volleyball on the sand.

In the old tavern, you could concentrate on the art of conversation. Not that the conversation was always that artful.

"Can I say something to you?"

"What?"

"You're pretty damn good."

"Thanks."

"No, I mean, you're pretty damn good."

"I know. I heard you the first time."

"What do you mean you know?"

"I just said, I heard you say it."

"Say what?"

"That I'm pretty damn good."

"You think you're pretty damn good?"

But at least you could hear it all. So also could you hear the fifth complete run-through of the game you'd just completed.

"Man, when you rounded third, I thought, uh-oh!"

"Why? I'm not slow."

"You're not *slow*?"

"No – am I?"

"Look, never mind. You made it, even though you were out."

"Bull*shit* I was out! Didn't you see that slide? Hooked the corner of the plate with my left toe?"

"Sure. And the ump called you safe, I know. I just know I wouldn't have sent you."

"Tell you what. You think I'm so goddamn slow, we'll go outside right now in the parking lot and have a race. Winner gets five bucks."

"Naw. You're drunk."

"*Drunk*! C'mon, I'll show you how drunk I am!"

"OK, if you say so. Let's just have one more beer first."

Nowadays, that level of discourse is rarely achieved. People may be saying something like that, but they can't be heard. In order for thoughts to be successfully communicated over the din, they have to be converted to shouted slogans of no more than three words. So you get tavern conversations, amid the plants and over the nachos, of the following type:

"What it is!"

"Fuckin' A!"

"Blue Jays!"

"Too much!"

"*Not*!

Oddly enough, when one of the participants in such a conversation is asked what he did at the tavern, he will say: "Oh, I was talking to Jim." The danger in the present situation is that soon he will believe he was. All conversation will be converted to monosyllabic grunts and repeated catchlines from television shows and what we will have to blame is the fact that drinking laws have been brought into the twentieth century.

As far as the life of the tavern is concerned, it may be that unnatural forms of behaviour have been imposed on it, a style of existence foreign to its nature. On the other hand it is nice to have carpets on the floor. On yet another hand, it means you have to take your cleats off before you can get a table.

Since the invention of loud music, much progress has been made in the development of gestures with which people can communicate in public places. These come in very handy at the modern tavern and many people who use them think that they are enjoying themselves.

How To Have Fun at a Tavern
Without Actually Saying Anything

1. Watch one of the ball games on television. When something exciting happens, point to the TV set. Then you and your friends can watch the replay together. When the replay is over, make the thumbs-up sign.

2. Wave at some friends across the room. Smile and pump your fist in the air.

3. Walk up to a friend and pretend to punch him, laugh, and give him the high-five.

4. Play a game of shuffleboard with a friend. If you win, point your index finger in the air, the Number One sign, then punch him on the shoulder.

How To Have Silent Fun
in the New Upscale Tavern

Not all taverns are sports bars. There are many other types,

some where extremely high-powered people, such as poll-
sters and officials of lottery corporations, hang out. No matter what the style of tavern, the music is the same. It is off
some service that plays only oldies, and it is loud. Still, you
can have fun, in some of the following ways:

1. Wave to a friend across the room. Point to your briefcase and pantomime telephoning him. He will do the same.
Having established that, wave to a friend across the room
on the other side of the room, point to your briefcase . . .

2. Spot a friend at the bar and slap him lightly on the back.
Smile and pantomime having lunch.

3. (For men only) Approach an attractive-looking woman,
smile, and give her your business card.

4. Motion a friend to follow you into the washroom.
Exchange fax numbers.

5. Circulate a piece of paper around the table upon which
each person enters his or her best guess on the next mortgage
rate.

6. (For women only) Borrow a match and start a bonfire of
business cards in the ashtray.

A good indication of the presence of the modern tavern in a
neighbourhood is the number of people standing on the
street conversing. If they are smoking, that means it is a *very*
modern tavern, one in which smoking is not permitted.
Whether they are smoking or not, it means they have
escaped the tavern in order to talk.

None of this should give you the impression that there is
no talk at all in the modern tavern. There are screams and
grunts and shouted slogans, as we have seen. And there are
also lulls between songs, in which things can be said. Now, as
before, certain expressions carry warning signs, signs that
say: "Get away from this person as fast as you can."

Things People Say in Taverns Which Should Be Followed Immediately by Your Saying "I Have To Be Going Now."

1. "Can I talk to you?"
2. "How're ya doing." (If uttered by someone who doesn't remember that he asked you how you were doing five minutes ago, and ten minutes before that.)
3. "What do you think *you're* looking at?"
4. "You know what the trouble with women is?"
5. "What do you *really* think of me?"
6. "Do you think I drink too much?"
7. "Want to know why I drink so much?"
8. "So, what's bugging *you*?"
9. "Here's my theory."
10. "You know what the trouble with you is?"

Another distinguishing feature of the modern tavern is the number of people in it who are not drinking. They may have given up drinking but not given up their affection for the place. They may be on a diet. Or it may simply be their turn to drink ginger ale and drive the others home. Whatever the reason, the modern tavern differs from its predecessor in that such creatures are no longer subjected to distrust and intense ridicule, as in:

"Hey, you think you're better than we are? Have a beer, for chrissake!"

People no longer say things like that because they are more sensitive or because the bottles all look so different these days they don't realize it's ginger ale in there. If they do notice, they might ask about it, in which case there are a number of answers you can give:

Five Reasons You Are Not Drinking

1. "I'm an alcoholic." There is a certain finality to such a subject. Spoken at a table in a tavern, it is likely to be

followed, in due time, by the statement "How about those Jays, eh?"

2. "I'm on a diet." Everybody understands that, everybody diets or thinks about dieting and nobody is threatened by it. And it is true, isn't it? Even if you intend never to drink again, that is sort of a diet, except that it's a permanent one.

3. "I'm in training." It is good to have something specific in mind when you say this, because people are certain to ask "For what?" And you can't really say, "It's a secret." The Boston Marathon always sounds good, but any nearby triathlon will do.

4. "It's just for Lent." Everybody has religious convictions of some type and everybody has a holy season they can cite. Be prepared for an earnest discussion of comparative religions, however, as the night wears on.

5. "It was getting in my way." Reflecting, as it does, an intense and burning ambition, this statement works better in upscale bars where when people get up to use the phone they get up to use their own. In an ordinary tavern, people are likely to say: "Getting in the way of *what*. You're getting in *our* way, you dumb shit!"

The non-drinker is a more familiar figure at the tavern these days and under less intense scrutiny now. Once they get used to you, people stop looking at you as if *you* were the one wearing the lampshade. And then, having dispensed with the preliminaries by giving a satisfactory explanation of the ginger ale, the non-drinker can have a reasonably enjoyable time at the tavern.

How To Be a Non-Drinker at the Tavern

1. Most people don't need to know the story of why you are not drinking. Just because you are not drinking doesn't mean you are not allowed to talk about baseball, the office, the

opposite sex, and comparative religions, just like everyone else.

2. You are allowed to win at shuffleboard, trivia, and all those other games. You don't have to apologize for winning and being sober. If the other people wanted to win badly enough, they could be sober too.

3. You need not apologize for being sober. Sobriety is a natural enough state. At any given time, many people are sober.

4. At the same time, don't feel that you have to remember everything that went on, just so you can tell your friends tomorrow. If they really want to know, they will ask you.

5. Don't think everyone is judging you because they think you are judging them. Most of them aren't thinking at all about the fact that you are not drinking.

6. A good way to make sure they aren't thinking about it is to stop whining about how much ginger ale costs. If ginger ale meant so much to you, you could stay home and drink it cheap.

7. Remember that seven ginger ales can make you feel about as bad as seven beers.

Perhaps the most important change wrought by the modern saloon is its attitude toward drunkenness. Suddenly, being drunk is not considered fashionable or even acceptable. Being drunk is a negative lifestyle attribute. The drunk is not a lovable and amusing character any more. The next day, instead of bragging about how drunk he was, the unfortunate fellow avoids the people he was with and hopes they are not talking about him. Only 15-year-olds brag about how drunk they were.

Why this change has occurred is not easy to pinpoint. It may have to do with society's dramatic opinion shift on drunken driving, now seen as worse than almost anything. The beer ads that dominate our television hours are also a factor. Although they portray beer as about the most stylish thing around, they also show a group of young men and women who are always cheerful, always lively, always alert. If beer commercials glorified the people grumbling to themselves in the corner, the people repeating their assertions on comparative religions, the people smoking two cigarettes, perhaps those people would find society more accepting of them. But society is not.

Still, the tavern is a place in which alcohol is served, and while drunkenness is not honoured, it will happen, even if by accident. It could happen to you. What then?

How To Be Drunk

1. Drunk people instinctively slow down. They think they are less likely to make mistakes and betray their condition if they do everything quite deliberately. That becomes a dead giveaway. Police look for people driving less than the speed limit. Friends notice the glass raised gradually to the lips, the stately walk across the living-room floor. You have a better chance of fooling people if you go fast – at least on foot. Better to move quickly, rush across the floor, quickly reach for the glass. When you stumble, when you spill, say: "Sorry. I guess I was in too much of a hurry."

2. We live in a society of hypochondriacs and pill-takers. It is just possible that your condition is not the result of having drunk too much, but of the way the drink reacts with your medication. And it is just possible that someone will believe that. Certainly, your saying so will trigger a round of conversation on what ails everyone in the room and perhaps you can sneak off and put some cold water on your face.

3. Don't thank people too effusively and more than once.

4. Try to avoid being sincere.

5. In the tavern, many odd things to eat are being served, any one of them capable of reacting oddly with your head or stomach and making you feel the way you feel. It could be

the chip dip, the salsa, the chicken wings, the tofu, even that purple and yellow thing you drank down in one gulp. Do they inspect those things?

6. Many people like to talk about their drinking when they are drinking. It is better to talk about the office.

7. A wise course is to say nothing at all. People may notice that and ask why you are saying nothing at all. Say: "I'm sorry, I'm just tired." If you can say that without saying: "I'm tired, I'm just sorry," people may accept it. This is a busy world. People work hard and play hard. They can identify with a person who is tired, especially if the person is only smoking one cigarette.

8. Above all, don't offer to tell people what the real trouble with them is.

9. The next day, don't ask people what you did, and don't apologize to anyone unless you are absolutely certain that you did something that needs to be apologized for. Sometimes an apology is necessary, but it can do more harm than good:

You: "I'm sorry about your carpet."

Friend: "Sorry about what carpet?"

You: "The one in your car. I, uh, was sick on it."

Friend: "No you weren't."

You: "Oh God. Whose car was it?"

10. If there was no doubt you were drunk and people ask you about it, say you were drunk. You might as well be honest about it. Also, if you admit you were drunk, people will know you don't have a drinking problem.

Chapter 15

The Video Store and the Impending Death of the Family

How To Find the Best Compromise Movie

Because it is a relatively new institution, no one realizes how important the video store is in modern society. In fact, few realize that the video store is an institution at all. But it is. It is tempting to call it the modern equivalent of going to the movies, except that going to the movies still exists as an institution. Like the movie theatre, the video store is where people go to talk about movies, except that at the real movies they talk about the movie they are seeing, whereas at the video store they have all seen it already.

The video store is where people go to seek amusement. It is where they go to keep up with popular culture. It is where families go to argue amongst themselves. And it may even be where boys go to meet girls, and vice versa. Sociologists have not picked up on that trend yet, but that is only because sociologists have had their heads down, searching in vain at the video store for movies about sociologists.

Not a single one has been made so far, although there have been many movies about psychiatrists and one about a very short painter in France.

Even the video store does not know it is an institution. It

has not yet adopted such institutional trappings as a code of ethics, an outside board of directors, or alphabetical order. Oblivious, so far, to its elevated position in the affairs of the people, unmindful of the fact that it plays a part in the Saturday night rituals of millions, the video store goes along much as it always has, selling memberships, putting the movies back on the shelves wherever there is a space, and slapping NEW ARRIVAL stickers on the latest teen monster flick.

Because it is a relatively new institution, not enough attention has been paid to the video store's importance and no code of conduct has been drawn up. People stumble into each other, not knowing how to behave, not knowing what they should be renting, not knowing what to say to each other, not knowing what their attitude should be to that alcove labelled ADULT over in the corner, particularly when they see the bishop emerge from it. Many questions arise, and they deserve answers.

Q. Why do I have to be a member of the video store anyway? I always said I wouldn't join any club that would have me as a member, or perhaps someone else always said that, but when I told them that at the video store they said I couldn't rent any movies. Is this fair?
A. Is what fair? Life isn't fair, so how could you expect a mere video store to be fair? The video store needs you to be a member so that it can keep track of the movies you rent and then let the police and unscrupulous reporters know what they are in case you are nominated to a high position. Everybody knows that. That's why you never see anybody in the ADULT section any more.

Q. What is the best way to strike up a conversation with a member of the opposite sex at a video store, if you know what I mean?
A. Anybody who has ever been to the movies knows that the

best place to strike up such a conversation is the art gallery. Think of the video store as the art gallery of the nineties. It is true that you can't rent pictures at the art gallery, but don't think of that. The thing to think of is that you can impress that certain someone with your great wit and erudition and vast experience, at least as it relates to renting movies. There are right and wrong ways to do this:

Wrong (to person holding movie): "Have you seen that one? It's great!" If the person had seen it, he wouldn't be holding it, unless he is one of those people who goes back and rents the same movie over and over again, in which case you don't want to have anything to do with him anyway.

Right (to person holding movie): "That one's pretty good, but his first one is better." Who can argue with this? Even if the movie is clearly identified with a woman, such as Marilyn Monroe, the "he" of "his first one is better" could be anyone – the director, the cinematographer, even Tony Curtis. Unless the special someone spots you for the phony poseur that you are, the line is quite effective.

Depending upon where you are in the store – the oldies, the comedies, the action films – other good lines should spring easily to mind. These include:

"Boy, you should see the gun he uses in that one!"

"I don't know; I like alienation all right, but not as a steady diet."

"It was all downhill after *Jailhouse Rock*, wasn't it?"

"Not only is it a great movie, but it's got some of Dexter's best playing on the soundtrack."

"A lot of people like his earlier stuff better, but I think his later, Bergmanesque stuff is really funnier."

"I can't figure out why they love him so much in France, can you? Dean Martin, though, *he's* underrated."

Other approaches are ill-advised:

"Excuse me? Do you know whether *Dirty Harry* is filed under D or H?"

"Do you know they've done a remake of that, with Barbra Streisand?"

"That one got three popcorn cups in *People* magazine."

"Excuse me, I couldn't help thinking to myself that you look like a Beta kind of person."

"Usually I abhor subtitles, but these are quite amusing."

"Do you know where I could find any films about sociologists?"

Q. Should movies be referred to as films? If I call them movies, does that mean I'm stupid?

A. The age of video has blurred the distinction between movies and films. Nowadays, the film by Godard sits on the shelf right beside the movie by Stallone. You can call them whatever you want. As a general rule, people who call movies films are looking for something about alienation, which they will be watching by themselves.

Q. There doesn't seem to be anything in the way of nutritious snacks for sale at my neighbourhood video store. Why is that, and is there anything I can do about it?

A. The enemies of nutritious snacks are always searching for new places to vend their unhealthy wares, such as red licorice and pickle-flavoured potato chips. It has been found that video store customers can be easily seduced into purchasing such unwholesome items. Eventually, with the release of more films in which people such as Clint Eastwood demonstrate a proper concern for nutritional values by eating carrots and yogurt, the video store will be conquered and the enemies of nutrition will attempt to establish a new beachhead somewhere else, such as at international aerobic chess competitions.

Q. I am not a bishop but I have a friend who is and he was doing some research in a certain part of a video store and

**when he came out of that part of the video store he was
noticed, whereupon people said to him such things as
"How dare you watch that smut?" and "I'm going to tell
the archbishop" – or at least so the story was relayed to
me. What should my friend have replied?**

A. Your friend has learned first hand an important video
store lesson – namely, that you are judged by what you have
in your hand, as the actress said to the – never mind. You
could be a bishop, you could be an electrician, a professional
hockey player, or a sociologist – it doesn't matter: If you are
found carrying *Wendi's Wet Weekend in Wales* around the
video store, you are forever known, not as a bishop, an electrician, a professional hockey player, or a sociologist, but as
the kind of guy who rents *Wendi's Wet Weekend in Wales*. Your
friend's only recourse, as a bishop, is to march up to the
counter and loudly demand that *Wendi's Wet Weekend in
Wales* be taken off the shelves immediately or he will call in
the authorities. If he hesitates to do that, he could try pretending that he thought it was a travelogue.

The video store's greatest potential for damage is that it
reveals to families how deep are the gulfs that divide them.
Early on in the history of video, the cry of: "Let's all go rent a
movie!" was often heard. Now it is not heard so much. What
is heard instead is: "Your father and I are going to rent a
movie," or: "Why don't you go rent a movie?"

This is because of what happens at the video store when
the entire family shows up. It is then that four people, say,
who usually get along, who manage to live in the same confined space fairly peacefully – these four people suddenly discover they have nothing in common, that they are waging
inner war.

Junior has headed straight for the section where all the
movie jackets have big guns on them. Sis is looking for a
refined comedy, perhaps something in French. Mum is

looking for a Gary Cooper movie she hasn't seen. Dad is over there talking in low tones to the bishop for some reason. Over the space of half an hour they will meet several times, carrying boxes, saying: "What about this one?" Each time someone will be rebuffed, and they will all leave eventually, either carrying four movies, each to be watched by a solitary viewer, or else carrying a much-debated compromise choice – a movie with no comedy, no big guns, no sex, and no Cooper, a movie that not one of them had the slightest interest in seeing when it was in the theatres, but which got good ratings from some magazine somebody dimly remembers.

The VCR was purchased as a way of keeping the family together, preventing it from flying apart on Saturday night, the children going their separate ways, Dad lying down in front of the football game, and Mum seeking peace and quiet elsewhere in the house. They would all rent movies and watch them together, become closer as a family.

The video store represents the betrayal of that dream, so far. It represents the sudden and sickeningly final realization that Dad is a Martin Scorsese person and Mum is a Frank Capra person, that Junior likes knives and Sis likes croissants. Yet the video store does not perish. It thrives, and increasingly is filled with people who come in by themselves.

How To Find the Best Compromise Movie

1. The following don't make good compromise movies: Westerns, films featuring Woody Allen, Bruce Lee, or Xaviera Hollander, anything by David Lynch, anything before 1950, anything with Lassie.

2. Slapstick is a good compromise. Mum and Dad can savour the irony of the pie-in-the-face. Junior and Sis can savour the pie-in-the-face.

3. The best compromise movies are disaster flicks. Each contains the following ingredients:

 a. Somebody like Paul Newman or Sean Connery.

b. Somebody like Jacqueline Bisset.

c. A cynical, sneering foreign person.

d. A fat person, often Shelley Winters, who is the first to die.

e. A gallant member of a minority group.

f. A weak and frightened person who is going to conquer his fear and save everybody's lives before perishing himself.

g. A great big storm or volcano or fire or wind or meteor or plague or tall office building that's going to wipe everybody out except Paul Newman and Jacqueline Bisset who will hug each other as the lava recedes but not before they have been saved by the formerly weak person and have conquered the sneering foreign person.

There are many important lessons for the whole family to be found in disaster movies, such as those about not sneering, not letting one's weight get out of control, being brave, and not trying to swim across a raging torrent in a 200-mile-per-hour wind. The family will unite in cheering against a common enemy – after all, nobody can root *for* a typhoon – and no one will have any difficulty following the plot.

Chapter 16

Culture: How to know what it is and get some for yourself

How To Be Hip – or Whatever the Hip New
Term for Hip Will Be

The Lambada: A Case Study

Country Music Appreciation for High-Rise Dwellers

What To Do When Both You and
the Rolling Stones Are Sixty

How To Film Festival

How To Survive Karaoke Night
with a Date Who Can't Sing

When Computers Go Bad

How To Accept an Award Gracefully Even Though
You Don't Know What It's For

What To Do If Royalty Is Around

The days have long since passed when you could have culture just by reading good books, wearing half-glasses, and going to the symphony and the opera. Nowadays everybody reads good books, or watches the TV adaptations. Politicians wear half-glasses. They also underfund the opera, causing it to disappear. Meanwhile, the symphony has been kicked out of the concert hall to make room for another six months of something like *Cats.*

In the future, you are going to have to look elsewhere for culture. Fortunately, our society has broadened the definition. Just about anything is culture, providing someone can write pompously about it in the newspapers and people in leather garments can talk about it on television.

Hence, rock music is culture. Graffiti is/are culture. Comic books are culture. Pornography is culture. Baseball cards are culture. All of which means that it is easier for you to have culture than it was for your ancestors. This is one of the triumphs of our modern North American society, making cultural the things that before were merely enjoyable.

It means that adults can go on enjoying the things they enjoyed when they were kids and still feel like adults.

If you'll remember, your parents had their popular music when they went to school – all that bobby-sox stuff. But it was always assumed that when they grew up they would put those old platters into the attic and take up Beethoven. They would sit in the living-room with Beethoven on the hi-fi and talk about that noise kids listen to today.

The process of throwing off childish culture could begin as early as university. Until the Sixties, it was assumed that university students would turn their back on the childish rock-and-roll music of their high school years in order to take up jazz and songs of the working man played on out-of-tune guitars. Also Beethoven. Around the time the Beatles arrived, that changed. All of a sudden it was all right to like rock music even if you were in university. And then it was all right to like rock music even past university, even to put rock music on your hi-fi and listen to it with your children.

No one knows who caused this, but it was a significant moment in North American cultural history, the day rock music became respectable. Given the lack of evidence to the contrary, it must be deduced that someone pronounced the music . . . *deep*. Once people knew the music was deep, then it could be listened to for its rich, harmonic, and lyrical deepness, rather than because you could dance to it real good after a few beers. For the generation coming of age in the sixties, the significance of this cannot be overstated: for the first time, the music they liked had become culture. The rock critic emerged, able to use big words to discuss the ineffable influence of Fats Domino on Jimi Hendrix. Professors wore T-shirts to class and discussed the ineffable influence of Walt Whitman on Bob Dylan.

After that there was no stopping culture. It was democratic

and accessible. Everyone could have it, just like half-glasses, which were now available without a prescription at the drugstore. And that is where we stand today, some three decades after the Beatles, a very cultured people.

We are also, however, a very competitive people, and there are those who resent the fact that everyone has culture now. That was the point of having culture in the first place – to set one apart from those who didn't have it. Now that everyone has it, the only way to set oneself apart from one's cultured fellows is either to have more culture, or to be the first to recognize and participate in new cultural forms as they appear.

How To Be Hip – or Whatever the Hip New Term for Hip Will Be

1. Ignore the media. The media are always trying to catch up with what used to be hip, except that they don't know that it used to be. They think it still is.

2. If you are involved in a cultural movement of any sort, such as a type of rock music or a style of painting, watch out for the arrival of the media. As soon as the first reporter arrives, move on. The first reporter will be followed by a camera crew and by other reporters and other camera crews, followed by the general public. There isn't room inside your tent.

3. It is true that when you move on, others will cash in on your movement by popularizing what you did when it was still hip, but there is nothing you can do about that, unless your lawyer says there is.

4. You could stick around and tell everybody you were there first, but what's the point? Did you ever see anybody given a medal for being there first?

5. You could attempt to freeze the rest of society out by adopting weird forms of dress, ridiculous forms of speech,

and disgusting personal habits. This never works. It will only be more popular.

6. You could pick something distinctively un-hip as your cultural avocation and hope that society ignores you and the mainstream flows around you. That did not work with country music, you will note. But some people have gone even further in, by becoming devotees of the music of Guy Lombardo and His Royal Canadians, for example. Even that is no guarantee of exclusivity, however.

a. A newspaper feature writer will write an offbeat story about a strange Guy Lombardo cult.

b. A television camera crew will appear.

c. Even if the general public does not catch on, there is a danger that your interest will be adopted by those who are seeking a means of expressing their ironic impulses. They will collect Guy Lombardo records as a means of showing that they are above collecting Guy Lombardo records, just as they now collect lawn ornaments as a means of showing their contempt for lawn ornaments. No one said it would be easy to be original.

7. In desperation, you could just like what you like and listen to what you listen to. At some point, you will suddenly be in vogue, and then, just as suddenly, you will not. And then, suddenly, you will again. The advantage of staying in one place, culturally speaking, is that you are by yourself most of the time.

It also pays to be a bit slow off the mark in adopting activities certified by the media as genuine crazes. Remember always that the media need crazes. Crazes fill up those dead spots at the end of newscasts. They provide subject matter for commentators and analysts. They cause the manufacture of equipment and outfits, which in turn can bring in advertising. None of this should be interpreted to mean that the media invent crazes. They don't. But sometimes they get a bit too excited too soon.

The Lambada: A Case Study

In 1989, a South American dance craze swept North America, apparently. To the untrained eye, it appeared to consist of men without shirts following women without skirts a bit too closely around the dance floor. The evening news proclaimed this a fad and it provided a good opportunity to show some pretty racy film footage. Magazines ran articles about the dance. Two feature movies were hastily produced. In one of them, a Brazilian princess used lambada dancing to save the rain forests. The lambada was taking over.

Or was it? Did you, an objective observer, ever see the dance performed, except on the news? Did you ever see anyone try it at a club or a party? Oh, you might think you saw it, but think again: wasn't that just Uncle Harry accidentally crashing into one of the bridesmaids?

Face it, the lambada sank like a stone because the only people who would do it were paid to – in movies and in live performances where it was known that cameras from the evening news would be present. Everybody else was too embarrassed, even those who had sunk hundreds of dollars into gaudy lambada outfits. There was, perhaps, a fear that someone would throw a pail of cold water on them.

What can we learn from this? Only that some fads have the staying power to become crazes (your yoyo still works, doesn't it?) and some don't. You can always wear your lambada clothes for Hallowe'en some time, although you will have to explain what you are dressed up as.

If the lambada has come and gone, the same can't be said for a number of cultural innovations. New forms of culture are constantly appearing and some of them stick. You need to know how to take part in them, or avoid them altogether, and which is right. Everybody knows how to behave at the opera, the symphony, the jazz club, the rock concert, the ballet – and if they don't know, the public library has many helpful reference books. But what of karaoke night, what of on-line computer porn, what of the local film festival? There is so much to learn and so little time.

Country Music Appreciation for High-Rise Dwellers

Country music has caught on with sophisticated urban people and it will not go away. This is because it is easy to understand, danceable, and rhythmic. Before, it used to be dismissed as something only unsophisticated rural people liked. That was a big barrier for sophisticated urban people. They had to keep their love of country music to themselves. Now country music is out of the closet, or the barn, or wherever it was kept. It is the music of beer commercials. Sophisticated urban people are allowed to like it, which means you now cannot escape it. So here are some things you need to know:

1. Country music is mostly about trucks and guitars. Although trucks are common in the city, they are not the kind of trucks country music is about. Country music is not about trucks that deliver washing machines to apartment buildings. Guitars are also pretty rare in cities. There used to be lots of them, but then protest music died and the guitar was stuck down in the basement somewhere. The first lesson in country-music appreciation is not to sweat the fact that you don't have a truck and can't find your guitar any more.

2. Country music is about hurtin'. Hurtin' is something like pain and something like stress and something like loneliness. If you put a "g" on the end of it, it is not hurtin' any more, it is something else, something you could probably get a bandage put on at the Emerg'. Often hurtin' results when someone's Baby runs off, leaving them alone, with the truck

and the guitar. This is a universal theme, and if you are to truly appreciate country music, you have to find a way of relating it to your city life. Suppose you had an excellent car, with sun roof, CD player, air-conditioning, power windows, and the whole thing, but no one would go out with you ever since you tried the lambada that one time – that would be hurting. It is not quite hurtin', although it might be if you dented your BMW a bit and got some mud on the carpet.

3. The reason city people like to identify with country music is because of the simple, basic emotions involved. Someone steals your truck and runs over your guitar and you're sad. Everyone can identify with that, and people like the idea that, no matter how complicated and technologically demanding their day-to-day lives are, they are still basically earthy, still capable of simple emotional responses, like cryin'.

4. Once you understand the concept of hurtin' and have a few albums, you are on your way. Country music playing on the CD in the car is somehow inappropriate; an old beat-up blaster in the kitchen is about right, so that you can listen to songs about trucks and guitars while you make the spinach salad.

5. City people don't talk much about country music yet. Unlike, say, jazz, there is not a lot of conversation associated with it, not a lot of "Who do you like on bass?" and that sort of thing. Mostly it is just a question of putting the album on the stereo, quietly, when company is around, and letting them all hurt quietly. Some of them may sing along as well, dropping "g"s.

6. Another major theme of country music is cheatin'. This distinguishes it from rock music, which is rarely about cheatin'. That is why teenagers are not big fans of country music. Teenagers, the main consumers of rock music, are still looking for that first relationship. There has to be lovin' before there can be cheatin'.

7. If you sense disapproval of your choice of country music and feel you must defend it, say that your interest is sociological. That suggests, to anyone but a sociologist, that you are making some kind of worthy sacrifice in order to have this music playing in your home. Only a fool would ask you to elaborate, but if asked to do so, mutter something about the cheating motif in twentieth-century popular art forms.

8. If you yourself disapprove of country music and find yourself in a place where it is being played, the best choice is to leave at once. Otherwise, you will make a smart remark and the next thing you know you will be hurtin'. If the country music is being played in a private home to which you have been invited, leaving is out of the question and silence is the best course. It is a lot better than asking if they have any Coltrane. If others are singing along and you don't know the words, simply put your head in your hands, as though it hurts, which may indeed be the case.

9. Pressed to say something about country music, a non-fan can draw upon a range of tested responses:

    a. "I had a guitar once. Only had three strings."

    b. "You can be lonely anywhere, can't you?"

    c. "Pasta and country music. It's quite a combination, ain't it?"

    d. "I've always thought the city was just the country with buildings."

    e. "She must have really lived."

What To Do When Both You and the Rolling Stones Are Sixty

1. At the concert, you don't have to stand in front of the stage any more. Get a reserved seat. You deserve it. You need it.

2. It is permissible to wear a 40-year-old tour T-shirt, but not necessary to offer the younger Stones fans your theory about the origins of the war in Vietnam.

3. Dancing is still fine, but get yourself checked out first. The knee is a tricky thing.

4. Complaining about the music being too loud will date you.

5. So will complaining about the music not being loud enough.

6. The concession stand may not have fruit juices. Best to bring your own.

7. There will be older people than you there. Show them some respect. They may be the only ones who still bring grass.

8. Be considerate in what you request: the Stones may not remember all their old songs.

9. Make a note of where you left the car.

How To Film Festival

Before the Information Age, there were film festivals because the commercial theatres were showing Elvis movies all the time. Typically, the film festival was run by a university professor with a big interest in film and enough budget to hire a couple of kids to run the projectors. Now it is run by a huge bureaucracy with a big public-relations budget, a media-relations office, and dozens of corporate sponsors. There are cocktail parties and awards and gala dinners and whatnot. Hollywood stars make appearances, as do noted film directors from foreign lands, although you may not have known they were noted before they made their appearances. All of this means that the film festival demands more of you than it used to.

You can still go just to see movies, but there are so many of them that it is possible to wind up in the wrong venue (as they say) and see that one about the wind in Iceland. It is important to remember that one of the reasons people go to film festivals is to talk about films, not just to see them. You may be called upon to converse about films at some stage and you want to do that without embarrassing yourself. In addition, there is a much greater choice than there used to be of things to avoid, and you want to make sure you take advantage of it.

1. It is all right to applaud at a festival venue, as opposed to an ordinary movie theatre, where, if you applaud, people think you are cuckoo. If you applaud after a film festival movie, it is because you understand and appreciate what the director was trying to do. Or at least it might as well be because of that. If you are at all timid, you might want to read up a bit first, to find out what the critics think are the films most likely to be applauded. Or you might want to wait until someone else in the venue applauds. If you are the bold type, you could risk being the only person in the venue who applauds. This will make people think you are the only one who understands what the director was trying to do. Or it will make people think you are a tourist.

2. Booing is riskier, especially if you are alone in doing so. People will expect you to justify your actions. And there is always a chance that the director is in the room.

3. Movies are called films and they are best referred to in abbreviated terms – such as *Wind* and *Kane* and *Oz*. If a movie already has a short title, such as M∗A∗S∗H, it can be referred to in a more indirect way, such as "Altman's Korean war film."

4. People leave films in the middle at film festivals. It is permissible to do so, even if it is only a case of wanting to get a bite to eat or hating the movie. If you want, you can fume out loud as you walk up the aisle, to make your departure more meaningful. Something like: "You call *that* cinematography?!?" is good. Most people will be too caught up in what the director is trying to do to notice.

5. Do you want to get to know the stars and directors and cinematographers who are there? Ask yourself this question:

Do they want to get to know you? How important is it to be able to say later to friends: "De Niro and I were chatting, when all of a sudden . . ." Better just to see the movie and get a good night's sleep, right? Still, if you are determined to meet famous people in the industry, there are certain things you should try to avoid saying:

a. "I've always wanted to know: What's a cinematographer do, anyway?"

b. "You know, at the end, when he says 'Rosebud,' what's that really mean?"

c. "Did you ever think of doing a Western?"

d. "Would your influences be, like, Fellini and people like that?"

6. In the theatre, never shout "FOCUS!" It is probably supposed to look like that.

7. After the film, remember not to talk about the plot. No one is interested in plots. Talk about the director and, if you can pronounce it, his oeuvre; talk about the cinematography, the scoring, the editing. Don't talk about the women, at least not in terms of how pretty they were. Never talk about the cars.

8. Holding your own in festival conversations will be better if you do not try to bluff. Pretending that you are a devotee of a particular Icelandic director is no longer a safe bet. In the Information Age, there are lots of people now who know all about Icelandic film directors. Even *early* Icelandic film directors.

9. The best thing to do is talk about the movies you really like, covering them over, if necessary, with a layer of something that sounds like critical analysis. Talk about the *mise-en-scène* of Mel Brooks, the horse motif in *Frankenstein* and *Saddles*, the phallic obsession in *Saddles*, *Frankenstein*, and even *Silent*.

10. Smuggle in your own red licorice. It is not usually part of film festival cuisine.

How To Survive Karaoke Night
with a Date Who Can't Sing

The modern cultural mood is participatory. You will recall that spectators at sports events no longer just sit there; they try to become part of the action, or at least part of the television picture. The same thinking has been applied to drinking establishments. No longer is it enough just to sit back, drink, and watch what other people do. Now you have to do things yourself. Even music. You do not sit there and listen to the music. You take part in the music. For you, the karaoke machine has been invented.

The karaoke machine is a microphone connected to a tape deck that has the background music to hundreds of tunes. You select the tune, the background music plays, and you sing the lyrics that appear on a screen, whereupon the mixture of your voice and the background music is, through the wonders of modern amplification, broadcast to the crowd, along with some videotape that has something to do with the song you are singing, in case the crowd gets tired, unaccountably, of looking at you.

Karaoke is modern capitalism's response to the fact that everybody thinks he's Sinatra after four beers. But suppose your friend is not. It's easy enough for you to refuse the microphone. After all, you *know* you can't sing. And you didn't come to this bar to have everyone look at you. But what about him. There he is, the background music to "My Way" is starting up, and he is about to rise from the table and seize the microphone. What are your options?

1. Say: "I'll give you ten dollars if you don't sing."

2. Tell him that you've been listening to the other singers and the sound system is distorting their voices something fierce.

3. Remind him that "My Way" is an extremely long song and ask him if he needs to go to the bathroom first. Then bribe the operator to take the machine away.

4. Say: "Wait a second! That's not your key!"

5. Take his hand, look him in the eye, and say: "I have to talk to you right now. I saw the doctor this afternoon."

Assuming none of this works and he sings, you can head immediately for the exit, which is the coward's way out, or you can stay and face the music. When he returns to the table, your goal is not to hurt his feelings, but not to encourage him too much either, in case he wants to try it again. And not to lie. Tell him:

1. "Nobody sings it like you."

2. "I'd love to hear you try something a little lower."

3. "I was watching the other people. They were spellbound."

4. "Can you shoot pool as well as you sing?"

In the best of all possible worlds, you get him out of there before he does further damage to his reputation or anyone's ears. In the worst of all possible worlds, you are forced to sing yourself. Much as you try to avoid it, there are certain situations in which you cannot turn the invitation down, such as if you are the boss at a company party, or you are entertaining an important group of Japanese clients and they have all sung already. The microphone is handed to you, the background music for "You Ain't Nuthin' But a Hound Dog" issues forth, and then what happens?

1. A reliable ploy is to turn the terror of technology to your advantage. Everyone in the room knows what it feels like when modern inventions don't work. They will understand completely when you open and close your mouth and no sound comes out of the speakers. It won't hurt to shake the microphone a couple of times and look at it suspiciously.

2. Also allowable is to wait for the introduction to be over, then announce into the microphone that it is Harry's birthday and lead everybody in a chorus of "Happy Birthday dear Harry," while you try to stick him with the microphone.

3. Something a bit more offbeat is to sing "Lady of Spain"

while the machine is playing "Hound Dog". Most people in the room will interpret this as satire.

When Computers Go Bad

The important thing, in the modern age, is not to let technology get the better of you. Just because a machine can do something doesn't mean you have to let it. And just because you can do something with a machine doesn't mean you have to do it.

Such thoughts spring to mind with the news, revealed early in the Nineties, that pornographic stories and even pictures are now available on computer bulletin boards. You may know that already and it may be perfectly okay with you, sitting up there accessing smut while everybody thinks you're updating the Christmas-card list. But for others, computer porn can be a problem. What happens, for example, when you are calling up different data bases, looking for stock market information, say, and your screen suddenly fills with dirty pixels.

1. You may be profoundly embarrassed, but you are unlikely to contract a disease, although your computer may pick up a virus.

2. The virus excuse can be tried if someone enters the room. "Look at this. I just turned on the drive and suddenly the words HA HA appeared and the screen began filling up with breasts."

3. Otherwise, hanging up immediately is not a bad idea. Unless you are a Canadian, you don't have to worry about hurting the feelings of whoever is asking you those dirty questions. If you want to be polite, simply input the words I HAVE A HEADACHE and then exit.

How To Accept an Award Gracefully Even Though You Don't Know What It's For

A major cultural development of the last decade is the rise in the number of awards that are given out for this and that. Award shows are seen as a good way of getting a particular art form – music or movies, for example – on television. The handing out of literary awards has been discovered to be a good way for corporations and communities to get their names in the news. Hence, the City of Brantford Literary Award will play everywhere and the Sani-Flush Second Novel Prize will attract lots of attention.

The guidelines for award participants are as follows:

1. Try to find out what status the award has. Asking how much cash is given out is obviously too crude. Usually the time and the place are good indications. If somebody says something about "squeezing it in during the lunch break," that would be one kind of indication. If the function is a dinner, that is better, but ask if there is a soup course.

2. In preparing your remarks, try to make them adjustable to the room and the augustness, or lack of it, of the occasion. In accepting the Mister Chili-Dog Award for Best Food Poetry, for example, it is probably not necessary to go into the contribution of your various elementary school teachers and how deeply touched you were by a letter you received the other day that you'd like to share with the audience here tonight. On the other hand, a black-tie audience at the National Arts Centre probably deserves something better than: "Um, you know, like thanks and everything."

3. As the meal progresses and the tension builds, try to get a sense of how important it should be to you to win the award. If people are, in general, strolling calmly to the stage, it ill befits you to leap to your feet, pumping your fist in the air when your name is announced, particularly if it is for one of the door prizes.

4. On a related subject, tears can be very moving. In fact, faking being overcome by emotion can get you out of having to deliver a speech. Still, there is a time and a place, and

winning the Dr. Scholl Award for Best Art Direction in a Shoe Commercial is not it.

5. Try not to refer to winning the award as "taking home the hardware."

What To Do If Royalty Is Around

Although currently in decline, the gala is still a major cultural force. People who can't think of anything constructive to do for the arts will pay huge amounts of money to dress up and have dinner with hundreds of other people who can't think of anything constructive to do either. Those who organize such events always attempt to get royalty to attend, for the extra cachet that brings, whatever that is. And royalty, whenever it is down on its luck, is likely to show up, if only for the eats. This means that if you can pay extraordinary amounts to eat hotel food, you could very well find yourself face to face with a member of the Royal Family. This is not easy, even for the Royal Family, which is used to eating out. How should you, a commoner in all likelihood, conduct yourself?

1. If you really want to meet the Royal People, you are on your own. Just remember that it is about the same as meeting famous film people: they won't remember you, whereas you will remember what you said later and feel silly. Also remember that men don't have to curtsey and women don't have to either any more because the monarchy has become more democratic, although you don't see any of them putting their careers on the line by running in elections, do you?

2. Remember that when you finally meet the Queen or the Princess or whomever, she will not know what to say to you. It is easier for you: you can say how glad you are that she has come to visit and isn't it good that the weather is so nice or isn't it too bad that the weather is so bad. But then, you are taking her lines. She can't ask you much about yourself because she is not consumed with desire to know much, or

anything – to be more precise – about you. She will not tell a joke, and if you tell one, you may have to explain the local references.

You: "Isn't it nice that the weather was so good, Your Majesty."

Her: "Yes, isn't it nice that the weather was so good."

You: "That's what I just said."

Her: "I beg your pardon."

You: "I just said that it was nice that the weather was so good."

Her: "Yes, isn't it?"

If it gets much past that, it will only be worse.

3. That is why the best thing to do at a royal gala thing is keep away from the Royal People. It is not hard to do. Watch where the crowd of people is and don't go near it. If you are seated and you see Royal People approaching, get up immediately and go to look for a phone.

4. Usually, evasive tactics will work fine, since it is unlikely that royalty will be chasing you around the room, unless royalty has absolutely nothing better to do. There is always the danger that someone you know, an important person, will volunteer to introduce you to the Royal People. Can you turn this offer down? Only in a few circumstances:

   a. You have a terrible cold and would hate to spread germs all over the Royal Family.

   b. You have just been informed that you are double-parked and are blocking the Royal Limousine.

   c. You have to leave immediately because you are being presented with the Sani-Flush Second Novel Prize.

5. In the unlikely event that a conversation cannot be avoided – for example, if you are seated next to the Queen at the head table and have to talk to her every other course – certain topics must be avoided:

a. Whether anyone in the family is contemplating divorce in the near future.

b. What it feels like to be on a stamp.

c. If there's anything she would rather do than be the Queen.

d. How much money she has in her purse.

Chapter 17

New Heroes of the Information Society

Why Your Child Should Be a Film Critic

How To Talk to a Television Anchorperson

Secrets of Hosting Your Own Fishing Show

Twelve Steps To Becoming a
Successful Self-Help Author

Secrets of the Competitive Aerobics Analyst

How To Be A Modern Politician

The Hardest Part of Being a VJ

Children's Music Faces the Challenge
of the Millennium

How To Be a Modern Voter

How To Have a Relationship with
an Infomercial Star

With changing technology, changing values, changing cultural forms, it is only natural that new role models in new occupations emerge. No guidelines exist for following in their footsteps, and no rules of etiquette exist governing relationships with such people. This is an attempt to fill that gap.

A preliminary observation: Because we live in the Information Age and because we are the kind of people we are, we place a high value on critics and commentators, people who describe things and assess them. We are less inclined to value people who actually do things, perhaps because there is less to do. The people who actually do things – make things, write things, perform, and compete – are certainly valuable, particularly to the critics and commentators, who would have nothing to say without them. So young people shouldn't give up on the idea of a future of actually doing something. Our society will need them, as raw material.

Why Your Child Should Be a Film Critic
This is the most coveted occupation in the modern world. More children today want to take up film criticism than any

other occupation. More children want to become film critics than want to become film-makers. This is quite understandable when you look at it. Why would you want to make movies and have critics yelling at you all the time about how flawed they are? Film criticism is an honoured occupation, more honoured with each passing year, and it has many other things to recommend it.

1. Free movies. This is what attracts people initially to the occupation, before they are bitten with the critical bug.

2. A chance to write and/or speak about what really excites you, although films will not excite you that much after the first couple of years.

3. The ability to perform a valuable public service. Without film critics, people might enjoy movies they shouldn't be enjoying and not notice the redeeming values in movies they thought they hated.

4. The chance to make lists, every ten years, of the best and worst of the decade. A chance to make lists, every one hundred years, of the best and worst of the century.

5. A chance to meet and talk with great film-makers and film stars. Many of them do not realize the extent to which their careers are proceeding in the wrong direction.

How To Talk to a Television Anchorperson

Most anchorpeople are anchormen. The reason they are called anchorpeople rather than anchormen is to disguise that fact. Television is very aware of the need for non-sexist language and any day now non-sexist policies will follow. The television anchorperson, along with the film critic, holds one of the most esteemed positions in modern society. Given the disrepute in which most government officials are held, the television anchorperson is as close to royalty as North America gets. But it is easier to talk to anchorpeople than to royalty, as long as certain conventions are observed:

1. Television anchorpeople are very important but

insecure. Jealous print journalists have drummed into their heads for decades the notion that anchorpeople are not real journalists, that all they do is read out loud, that they were hired for their looks. Therefore, when meeting a television anchorperson, it is always good to ask his or her opinion on some complicated issue, in case he or she has one.

2. Never ask, "Who does your hair?" or, in the case of a male anchorperson, "Who does your teeth?"

3. Similarly, never ask, "Who writes your stuff?"

4. Saying "I really think you read so well" is not as flattering as you might think.

5. A good way of starting a conversation is to ask anchorpeople about the personal danger they have experienced in covering stories. Anchorpeople like to think of themselves as covering stories and a recent journalistic trend is to have them flown right to the scene of hotels near major war zones.

6. Anchorpeople are not eager to answer questions about what the weatherperson is really like.

7. People in any profession like to think that a great deal of mystery surrounds the mechanics of their job, and anchorpeople are no exception. Ask if the little screens on the desk are two-way and if the correspondents out in Asia and wherever can see the anchor desk. Ask how there is always just the right amount of news every day to fill up the time.

Secrets of Hosting Your Own Fishing Show

As television expands into more and more cable channels and as viewing audiences become more and more fragmented, new figures command the spotlight. One such is the fishing show host, an increasingly compelling personality, seen each week on Saturday afternoon TV and live at fishing tournaments across the continent.

1. What you need:
   a. A boat with chairs in it.
   b. A rod and tackle box.

    c. A video camera.

    d. Someone to talk to.

    2. One key to a successful fishing show is catching fish. But they need not be caught all at once. Videotape can be edited so that only those moments in which a fish is actually on the line will be presented to the home viewing audience.

    3. Another important element is pretty pictures. Obviously there will be water in the picture, which is a good start. But if all the viewer sees is water, that will be boring. There should be scenery – trees and swamps and cliffs and things like that. The fishing-show viewer is stuck in the city on Saturday afternoon and wants to be taken away from it all. Therefore, it is advisable not to have billboards, parking lots, and utility poles visible in the picture.

    4. Few people think of fishing shows in terms of writing, but believable dialogue is an essential ingredient, to underline the excitement of fishing. Bad writing can completely destroy the mood. Here is an example of bad fishing-show dialogue:

    "I wonder why we haven't caught anything?"

    "I don't know. We didn't catch anything yesterday either. Maybe we should change lures."

    "We've already tried them all."

    "Maybe we should go back."

    "No, let's keep our lines in the water, at least until the half-hour is up."

    "Got the net ready?"

    "I don't know. Did we bring one?"

    "I wish it would stop raining."

    5. Good fishing conversation is never improvised. It is true that it has a kind of improvisational quality to it, as if the participants, usually two men, are just saying whatever comes into their heads. But, in fact, it must be planned down to the second, with dialogue prepared for each possible situation. When it works, it sounds so easy . . .

"What've you got on there?"

"That's the green spoon. Wow!"

"What, a fish?"

"She's a good one. Let me just . . ."

"I'll get the net."

"Ooo-ee!"

"All right!"

"She's pulling hard."

"The net's right at my feet."

"You give them just a bit of slack and they take off on a run."

"Still there?"

"Get the net."

"I've got the net."

"Nice fish."

"He getting close?"

"She's getting close."

"I've got the net."

"Good fish."

"I've – got him."

"Nice fish."

Twelve Steps To Becoming a Successful Self-Help Author

Various phobias and allergies, along with overweight, under-weight, and many addictions, are now available in book form. The authors of such books have been successful in helping readers recognize that they had problems they didn't know they had, and just in time to buy a book too. If you have a word processor and your life has been just the slightest bit unhappy, you have a chance to join the ranks of self-help authors, a powerful cultural force in our society. Here's what it takes:

1. You have to have suffered, or know someone who has, or have read widely.

2. You must have the perceptiveness to recognize that such outwardly harmless conditions as left-handedness, short eyelashes, and dry skin are in fact burdens that can be cured if only the reader can learn to develop and focus his self-pity and cough up $27.95 for the book.

3. You must have the creativity to understand that being the *child* of someone with short eyelashes or dry skin can cause suffering as well, and is treatable.

4. You must be able to recognize who is to blame for your suffering. Caution: some people blame themselves for the things that go wrong in their lives, but this makes for boring reading. Plus, it is axiomatic that people will not lay down good money to find out that their troubles are their own fault.

5. Many problems in life are the result of not being hugged enough as a child. This may not be precisely true in your case, but you can't go wrong in suggesting it. If, as the result of your book, people do more hugging, where's the harm?

6. There must be at least ten steps to remedy the problem, and twelve is popular. Some trail-blazing authors have got the number of steps up to more than twenty, and the unofficial record is thirty-three.

7. You may be tempted to solve the problem in five steps or fewer, or in five minutes, but that makes for a short book. In addition, solving the problem too quickly and too definitely means that a sequel has less chance of selling.

8. The most popular and most sure-fire villains are parents, although society as a whole can always take some of the blame. As the number of problems for which blame can be attached grows, the field is widening and it is now possible to finger the schools, the church, the government, and even Martians for whatever your problem is. If your parents are Martians, you have a best-seller and probably a sequel as well.

9. The key to getting readers to hate their parents is to

convince them, ever so gradually, that they are truly unhappy, even if they didn't think they were. They must learn that their happy times are in fact periods of denial. Once they are convinced that their lives are miserable, they will be more likely to hate those who had a hand in it.

10. Inventing extra steps is often necessary when you get stuck at nine.

11. Being able to weep real tears on television when discussing your book is an important asset. Television is the perfect vehicle for suffering, and the camera loves tears. Don't be afraid to cry. Tears are a definite sign of sincerity. No one will buy a book written by someone who is not sincere.

12. Never stop at eleven steps when you have a shot at twelve.

Secrets of the Competitive Aerobics Analyst

As we have seen, there is no activity that cannot be made competitive and there is no competitive activity that cannot be televised. Any televised activity requires people to do the play-by-play and it also requires analysts – experts to talk during the periods when nothing is going on and tell the viewers when the people doing the competing are not performing as well as they should.

The practice is as old as figure-skating. It continues through beach volleyball, free-style skiing and monster truck competitions, and it comes to rest at competitive aerobics. Soon, something really absurd will come along.

Aerobics is, or are, exercise. You do the exercises, your heart and lungs do some work and get stronger. That was the idea. Somehow, through the wonders of the modern age, an economic culture developed out of this. Fashions were designed, music was added, dance routines were developed, and, the next thing you know, there they all are in Tokyo, competing in the pairs competition for the Suzuki World Cup and smiling constantly. It doesn't look like exercises. It looks like dancing. But expert aerobics commentators would know the difference and in conveying it would follow the Rules of the Esoteric Sports Analyst:

1. The word "it" is your friend.

"Look how he goes high with it."

"She took it halfway around that time then brought it back." No one has to know exactly what "it" is. You don't even have to know yourself. Pioneering uses were by Olympic diving analysts, who invented the phrase: "She really puts it in this time," meaning, as far as anyone could tell, that she went into the water, but serving, on a deeper level, to separate the dive – "it" – from the diver – "she."

2. Analysis in new sports, such as competitive aerobics, does not have to be critical. The theory is that the audience would like to be told how good each routine is. Once the dive has been separated from the diver, the aerobics move from the aerobic mover, it is easier to be critical without sounding cruel. "It looks like that one got away from him a bit" sounds nicer than "Look how clumsy he was."

3. Any sport needs jargon in order to be capable of analysis. The analyst needs words he or she can use and seem to understand that are not commonly understood by the average viewer. That creates a distance between the analyst and the viewer, establishing the analyst as an expert and the viewer as some clod gawking at people in bathing-suits. Figure-skating came of age when the double axel was discovered – the term, not the move; professional football, as a sport worthy of analysis, was nothing until analysts could differentiate between the strong safety and the weak safety. Baseball for years was thought of as a game everybody could understand until the revelation that the ball had rotation. It is early yet for competitive aerobics but certain tendencies are discernible:

"It's also important in the pairs competition to have good use of the space. All those transitions are important."

Any activity with transitions has a good chance of lasting.

4. Good analysis need not be esoteric. Certain concepts, such as "clean," work in almost any context. "Their technique is very clean" has a nice authoritative ring to it without overburdening the audience with specifics. Directions can also be invoked effectively, as in: "She should get a little lower in that push-up, though." When you think about it, everything could be a little lower or a little higher than it is.

How To Be a Modern Politician

Despite the public pummelling politicians take, there are people who decide to become politicians anyway. It may be that an elected post might look good on their résumés later on. Or it might be something as simple as wanting to serve their fellow people. Who knows? Every year, despite all odds, despite the inevitability of defeat, the near-certainty of being attacked in the media, even the possibility of having past adventures, romantic or otherwise, plastered all over the television screen, otherwise sensible individuals throw their hats into the ring. Some of them even have to go out and buy a hat first.

Such people deserve advice, all the advice they can get. Anybody, after all, can be a banker or a hairdresser, live a life in which mistakes are never a matter of public interest, a life that never needs to present itself to the voters for permission to continue. Would you go before the people every four years and let them decide whether you can have another four years at the bank?

The two most difficult things a politician must deal with are ideas and voters. Ideas are nothing but trouble and the modern politician avoids them as much as he can. One of the biggest mistakes a politician can make in the modern democratic age is to have an idea. As soon as a politician makes the mistake of expressing an idea, the opposition jumps on it and ridicules it; the press picks it up, analyses it, comments unfavourably upon it in editorials, and organizes man-in-the-street polls in which ordinary voters say it's the dumbest idea they've ever heard.

As for modern voters, they appear in menacing clusters – the association of this and the coalition of that. Voters are interest groups and interest groups are votes. They are also money. For you, the politician, your entire existence is reduced to one consideration: Are you for them or against them?

Are you sure you want to go ahead with this? If so, here's what you need to know:

1. Always look people in the eye. Stare at them if necessary. Real people don't look each other in the eye all that much, but everybody has read that politicians who don't look you in the eye are sneaky.

2. Don't smell of whisky or cologne. In person, people don't mind that too much, assuming you are not severely drunk or severely fragrant. But people will talk. They will tell their friends that they have met you, and their friends will want to know their impressions: "She smelled of whisky," people will say, not being able to think of much else, or "He smelled of cologne." Cologne on a man is about as bad as whisky on a woman. Whisky on a woman suggests that she hangs out with politicians, something that people would prefer to think she was above doing. Cologne on a man suggests that a man took the trouble to think about fragrance, something male voters never like to think of themselves as worrying about, especially if they do.

3. Shake hands firmly but not too firmly. If you shake hands too firmly, people will think you are disguising a weak grip. That is the kind of intensive scrutiny politicians get. If one person tells another you have a strong handshake, the other person will say: "Strong handshake? *Uh*-ohhhh."

4. If you are talking to a voter named Bob, remember his name but don't put it into every sentence. As in: "You know,

Bob, the voters are telling me that this big-government issue is uppermost in their minds, Bob." If people hear you putting their name into every sentence, they think you are trying to sell them something, which you are. Also, not working too hard with the name can save you some embarrassment:

"You know, Bill, the people are fed up with high taxation, Bob."

5. When the Association For This and the League Against That come to call, your safest choice is abject surrender and complete support for their position, even if the position of the two groups is entirely opposite. The alternative is to have your opponent win their endorsation in the election and have thousands of dollars put into the campaign for the express purpose of making sure you don't win. It is a bit cowardly, sure, to support every interest group that comes to call, but once people realize that you have supported many groups that have diametrically opposite positions, they will realize that your support doesn't count for much and will leave you alone next time. If the Association For This tries to defeat you, then the League Against That will come to your assistance. Or at least *someone* will. Heaven knows, you've supported enough of them.

6. In dealing with the media, never use the expression "off the record," unless you are certain that you want the information made public. Reporters are taught that off-the-record information is the most valuable there is and will do their damnedest to get the information into their stories. Ordinary voters love to hear stuff that is "off the record" because it suggests you are sharing a confidence with them. Just make sure the information isn't really confidential.

You: "Off the record, Bob, I think we have a pretty fair chance of winning this thing."

7. Make sure everyone knows that you are not a politician and that the reason you entered politics is because you hate politics. If you happen to be ignorant about the way politics

operates, brag about it. In the modern democracy, ignorance of politics is considered a virtue, especially among politicians. (Note: This does not work everywhere in society. For example, if you have become a doctor, do *not* advertise the fact that you hate medicine and don't know anything about it.)

8. Attack other politicians for being politicians. "My opponent insists on playing politics with the issues." There is nothing inaccurate about this, for a start, and it plays to the bias most people have, in the modern democratic age, about politicians. Exactly who they want to have involved in politics, if not politicians, is difficult to know. The sad fact is that they feel that way and you want to avoid the image of being a politician. You are just a lawyer, or whatever you were, who accidentally won a nomination. If you happen to be an incumbent with years of experience in office, you obviously lack all of the main criteria for being elected and are dead meat.

9. There is no sure-fire way to respond to a slur. Even if the slur is not true, an angry denial ("I did not take her to Disney World on the government jet!") only prolongs the debate and makes people aware of the original slur who were not aware of it in the first place. Remember that there are a lot of those. At the same time, the urge for revenge is almost irresistible. Say: "There are some things I could say about my opponent's past, but I won't because I think the issues here are more important than playing politics." Whatever you are, you are not a politician, right? And will your opponent demand to know what things you could have said about him? Not likely.

10. If you have an idea, be wary of advancing it too blatantly. The media and your opponents will recognize that you have an idea. They will attack it and your career will be over. If you have to put forward an idea, for some reason, get

a pollster to float it out to the public. If the poll results are favourable, advance it as an idea that sprang from the people. The people might like it better then and you will not have to take the rap for it if it is no good.

The Hardest Part of Being a VJ

The rise of the rock video culture has brought with it instant visibility for what are known as vjs or video jockeys. For the most part they act like radio disc jockeys in front of a television camera – introducing the next song, breaking for commercials, reading requests, and that sort of thing. None of that is too hard. The hard part is when rock stars show up at the studio and have to be interviewed. Being a rock star means you don't have to be polite or even articulate when being interviewed. To make matters more difficult, most rock bands like to be interviewed all together, which means that the vj has to contend with four or five people all at once who lack the commitment to be polite or articulate. They will be making private jokes and giggling amongst themselves, nudging and interrupting one another and wandering off camera.

VJ: "I'd like to ask you –"
Star 1: "She'd like to ask us."
Star 2: "Haw haw."
Star 3: "What's this, anyway?"
VJ: "That's the camera. And I'd like to ask you –"
Star 2: "Haw haw."
Star 1: "Uh."
Star 3: "Where's Billy gone to?"
VJ: "I think he wandered off the set. I don't know why."
Star 1: "She doesn't know why!"
Star 2: "Haw haw."

The vj interview is still a fairly new art form, but certain principles can keep it from getting completely out of control.

1. Asking about the music is iffy. Asking about the video is better. Rock musicians know all about how videos are made.

2. A good safe question is the tour the group is on now. Most groups are good at naming cities and can remember where they were yesterday and where they will be tomorrow.

3. An even better topic of conversation is image. Groups realize how important image is to their hopes of success and are well versed on image matters. While there may not be a reason for everything they sing, there is a reason for everything they wear.

VJ: "When did it start, this thing about wearing all your clothes sideways?"

Star 1: "It's just a thing, you know. Like one day we were all talking and someone said 'Sideways' and that was it."

Star 3: "It was him. He said 'Sideways.'"

Star 2: "Haw haw."

VJ: "Is it hard, getting dressed sideways?"

Star 1: "Not really, once you get used to it, like putting your leg where your head usually goes."

VJ: "I guess your fans are really getting into it in a big way."

Star 3: "Yeah, man. We get letters all the time. Even from the parents. They go 'My kid can't put on his pyjamas in less than like an hour because of you guys.'"

Star 2: "But that's ok. We can take criticism. Groups have endured persecution before."

4. The subject of persecution is a good one to follow up. Rock stars love to talk about politics – South Africa, whales, and kids being hassled for daring to show a little individuality in where they put their arms with regard to the various holes in their shirts. Rock stars also like to talk about how people shouldn't be ashamed of their bodies and how it is wrong to censor satanic messages heard on records played backwards.

Children's Music Faces
the Challenge of the Millennium

It is not true that more children are being born than ever before. It is true that today's children are being raised more solemnly than any previous generation and their parents are more attentive to every aspect of their upbringing. We can thank the Information Age for this too. Because so much is known about early childhood education, about mental health in childhood, about socialization, about diseases, about theories of play and theories of conflict, the children are under a microscope, put there by parents who want to make sure they are perfect.

That's why not just any music will do. Music needs to serve a purpose beyond giving children something to hum and tap their feet to. Music must give them the proper attitudes toward their neighbours, their teachers, their schools, their environment, their diet. Entertainers who can provide that – provide the right songs – are in demand. It is a growth industry and a potentially competitive one. Songs must be more than collections of nonsense syllables and jokes about giraffes.

You may resist that. You may think it is still enough to sing inkalarinkydinkydo and whatnot. But others are waiting in the wings, with their giant stuffed animals and politically correct marionettes. If you falter, they will drive you out. It is a giraffe-eat-giraffe world.

Can you be a successful children's entertainer in the Information Age? The odds are against you, unless you try really, really hard.

1. Remember, it *is* the Information Age. That means children know just about everything. So little songs about adding and subtracting and how thirsty a cactus gets are going to receive hundreds of tiny little yawns.

2. You still have to smile, though. Parents have taught their

children that adults who don't smile are the kind of adults you shouldn't tell where the mall is if they stop you on the street.

3. On the other hand, kids know that adults who smile too much are phonies. So you have to strike a balance.

4. It is true that you are singing to entertain the kids, but never forget that it is the parents who buy the albums and the tickets. The tunes should make the little kiddies tap their feet; the words should make the adults feel their children are learning valuable lessons, thereby saving the parents a bit of time in their busy lives.

5. For that reason, a big laser light show is probably not too great an idea. The kids will love it, but the parents will worry about tiny ears and eyes.

6. As in other forms of activity, it pays to read the papers. There are important new topics that have not had children's songs written about them yet, such as Nice Mr. Condom and Bad Mr. Cholesterol.

7. Friendship and brotherhood and loving animals and not littering have all been done. But there have been few children's songs on the themes of co-dependency so popular in our times. That may be a direction worth taking in writing children's songs – finding someone for them to blame for the fact that they feel sad or their footsie hurts.

> *I wish my Daddy wasn't left-handed,*
> *I wish my Mommy didn't golf.*
> *Sing bickety boo;*
> *Bickety bickety boo.*
> *It's giving me all kinds of problems*
> *That I don't know how to solf.*
> *Why can't my parents be normal?*
> *I'm sorry I ever knew them.*
> *Sing rickety rickety roo;*
> *Rickety rickety roo.*

My future life is ruined
And I think I'm going to sue them.

How To Be a Modern Voter

The discovery of the political centre was a landmark event for politicians. It gave politicians a place to stand where voters wouldn't vote against them for being left or right.

It was not long before every politician tried to be in the centre. Once there, they realized that the ideas they had previously held, about public ownership, about free enterprise, about high interest rates and low interest rates, about rights of unions and rights of capital, were ideas unsuited to life in the centre. They would have to be jettisoned.

At the same time, high-powered research told politicians that voters like the *idea* of politicians having ideas, even though they might not like the ideas themselves. So politicians and their researchers set to work developing a set of statements that resembled ideas but would not alarm anyone. A partial list follows:

1. "We need a government that listens to the people."
2. "We must put aside fear and show confidence in the future."
3. "A changing world poses new challenges."
4. "The hope of the future is in our young people."
5. "We must uphold the principles handed down to us by the founders of this great country."
6. "There are no easy answers."

When you, as a voter, hear one such idea expressed, it means that the person who expresses it does not have an idea and is no danger to you. But there still exist, it is rumoured, politicians who have ideas. You might want one to represent you, or you might have to avoid such a person altogether, as being likely to cause controversy. In either case, it is good to be able to recognize the warning signs:

1. Politician doesn't agree with everything you say.
2. Politician doesn't know results of latest poll.
3. Politician doesn't call you by first name.
4. Politician doesn't say your children are beautiful.
5. Politician makes statement before television cameras arrive.
6. Politician continues speaking after television cameras leave.
7. Politician doesn't use words such as "dynamic."

As we have seen, the modern politician will take a position on the issue of whether his opponent is avoiding taking a position on the issues. As far as taking a position, that's about as far as it goes. You, as a voter, could demand something more than that, but, if you do, make sure your candidate has a strong handshake and looks you right in the eye.

How To Have a Relationship with an Infomercial Star

The infomercial has come of age, or will soon, if someone does not ban it first. This is the thing that you find on your TV set after midnight when you are looking for a late movie and instead see a vaguely familiar face hosting what looks like a panel discussion. Other familiar faces are on the panel and as you listen, you gradually come to the realization that the subject of the panel discussion is how great a certain type of pillowcase is.

Each panelist describes the great things that have happened in his or her life since becoming converted to the pillowcase. The studio audience applauds. More guests are brought out, each talking admiringly about the pillowcase. There are questions about the pillowcase from the audience and each elicits a response to the effect that the pillowcase is just terrific. The response is applauded. An 800 number is shown. The audience applauds. Film clips are shown from time to time in which ordinary people talk about how great the pillowcase is. Then, half an hour later, the show is over and another one starts – another panel discussion, or something that looks like a public-affairs program, about how great sunglasses are, or stop-smoking devices, or cosmetics, or a system for making lots of money.

To say that such programs have come of age is simply to acknowledge that there are now awards shows for people involved in infomercials. Awards are given for the best director, the best performance, the most innovative product, the best performance by a celebrity.

All of this makes it a growth industry and increases the chance that you may, some day, enter into a relationship with someone who happens to be involved in the infomercial industry. Can true friendship flourish with such a person? Only if you keep certain things in mind.

1. Conversation is a bit different from the ordinary. Instead of beginning with the weather or the Edmonton Oilers, you must say something like: "I just discovered this exciting new product!"

2. People are likely to stop your friend on the street and you should be prepared not to laugh at them. They will tell your friend that they quit smoking, lost eighty pounds, made $20,000 in the first week, or had the best sleeps ever. It will be hard for you to compete for your friend's attention, particularly if you run out of exciting new products.

3. A few such encounters with the public and you will know enough not to make cracks about the kind of people who are in your friend's studio audience. They love exciting new products too, and let's try to leave it at that.

4. To make sure your friend telephones you, try to get an 800 number.

5. Try to figure out if your friend likes to talk shop, or if he is the type who prefers to leave the office at the office. Even

though you are dying to know what parts of the program constitute the program and what parts constitute the commercial, don't force the subject if you sense he would sooner talk about something for which there is no televised cure, such as volcanoes.

6. Never ask if your friend has had any offers to do *real* television.

7. If you are feeling down, keep it to yourself. Your friend hears nothing but positive thoughts at work and will have difficulty coping with anything else. Hearing that you are blue, he may try, in desperation and with the best of intentions, to sell you something.

Chapter 18

The Future and How To Avoid It

Leisure and Culture in the Exciting Years Ahead

Your Future Home: A Cineplex with a Back Yard

Thawing Uncle Harry: Dos and Don'ts

Outer Space: An Imperfect Solution
to the Parking Problem

Dos and Don'ts of Weightless Flight

How To Have a Meaningful Conversation
with an Extraterrestrial

The future will be here any day now. The thing is to know what parts of the future you want to hide from when they get here. And to do that you have to know what's coming.

Some of it is here already, disguised as the present. For example, Canadian entrepreneurs are crossing the country scuba-diving in golf course water hazards for golf balls that they can resell. The first golf course water hazard scuba-diving fatality has already happened. There will be more of this activity as more and more agricultural land is turned into golf courses. Some projections indicate that used golf balls may, within twenty years, be our leading agricultural crop.

Another element of the future that has already arrived is interactive television. It is mostly featured in bars so far, but soon will spread into homes, making it possible for ordinary people to dictate what camera angles they would like to see and to compete with others in guessing what play the quarterback will call. The interactive TV of the future will be far more sophisticated – the viewer will be able to push a button during a drama and cause the story line to include a lengthy driving sequence, during which the screen will fill with scenery, nice music will play, and the viewer can go make a sandwich. The net effect of interactive TV will be to create a generation of active viewers who are so active being viewers that they will have no time to act.

The presence of the future is also evident in several new products, one of the most interesting of which is called the SwimEx. The SwimEx is a large bathtub in which the lucky owner swims against a moving current of water, the moving current capable of being adjusted as to speed and temperature. Says an advertisement, "You get all the benefits of swimming, without ever leaving home."

Will it be worth leaving home in the future? You will have to, if you face the wrong direction in your SwimEx and the moving current of water causes you to bash your nose on the other end of the pool. Hospital visits aside, indications are that many people, despite the growing attractions of the home, despite the disappearing ozone layer and whatnot, will be venturing out every day. As a consequence, it is possible to predict that our most important economic resource in the years ahead will be parking spaces.

In fact, the economy will be based primarily on parking. Parking and information: and much of the information will be about parking. Another major industry will be software for managing the information. The cities will continue to grow and people will go to work in huge office buildings where they will manage, share, and distribute information. The information the information sector works on will be about the information sector itself, because of its sheer size and importance and the number of people employed in it, and about parking, which will become increasingly valued as more of it is taken away to make room for huge office buildings to house more information workers.

Not all other forms of economic activity will disappear. Agriculture will be gone, of course, sacrificed for golf courses and the bounties of the golf ball harvest. Food will be imported from Japan in a miniaturized form for which the information sector will produce recipes. One of the few occupations that will continue is film criticism, its ranks swollen by a glut of late-twentieth-century recruits. The glut of film critics will necessitate the survival of the film industry, to provide something for the critics to work on. Many of the new films will be about parking, such as the legendary *Lethal Parkade II*.

There will be work for interactive TV critics – that is, critics of interactive TV – its practitioners suggesting to viewers what endings they should have chosen for the interactive programs they watch. By criticizing their choice of endings, the critics will be setting in motion a chain that will end with their being able to criticize readers directly, without even the need of a film or TV program as pretext.

An important element of the information sector will be the development of new software to be used at home by those who cannot, or choose not to, park. Such software will enable them to partake of the vast amounts of new information available and to perform complex chores without leaving their homes – shopping, going to the library, and worshipping, through interactive call-and-response software such as Vespers 5.2, at the church of their choice.

As parking becomes more and more important, the government will step in and establish a Department of Parking, with a subsequent bureaucracy and the issuance of regulations. These will be examined by the media and attacked by the opposition, and the political process will continue very much as before, with the exception of the major debates being about parking rather than constitutional matters. A future controversy will be over free parking with the United States.

With the growth of the bureaucracy it will be demanded, from time to time, that huge office buildings be torn down to make room for the bureaucracy to park. And it will be argued, in opposition to the demands, that the need for more parking spaces cannot be met without an increase in the regulatory capacity of the government, which will mean more people and more office space and more parking for the office spaces.

Inevitably, some golf courses will have to be destroyed.

Many pages ago you learned how to amaze your friends with parking anecdotes. The future is going to demand even more of you. Since parking will be everyone's occupation, as well as their preoccupation, it will be more difficult to sustain an audience. It is possible that talking shop as we know it will disappear and that people will want to talk about something else entirely, to get their minds off parking. That is where you will have a distinct advantage if you can talk about how many kilometres you swam in the bathtub last night.

Buying a bathtub in which you can swim will be pretty much as it is today, except that it will be a televised hologram of a salesman bragging to you about how many gallons you can get per mile. The financing of it will be different, however. By the time the future arrives, all bank lending will be done by machine. At first, this will mean only that a machine is programmed to say "no," but increased sophistication will be brought to the lending machine as banks realize they are losing customers to video stores and their growing lending operations. Eventually, bank machines will be programmed to ask you a series of questions, such as whether it will take you a long time to repay the loan, whether you are in possession of several major credit cards, and whether you are already deeply in debt. If you answer "yes" to all questions, the machine will approve the loan.

In the future you will be able to do all this without leaving your home because of the development of sophisticated home financial software and accompanying programs, such as Home Bankruptcy. This will cut somewhat into bank activities. However, the bank will welcome the extra time available to prepare itself for Hallowe'en.

One response to an economy based on parking may be an increased tendency to withdraw from participation. This tendency, visible on a small scale in the early nineties, is called cashing out. People involved in cashing out decide that they do not want to become rich and famous, that they want to work less rather than more and live less demanding rather than more demanding lives. That will continue in the future, with more people working part-time, spending more time with their children and earning extra money in crafts, such as sculpting things out of old golf balls.

Leisure and Culture in the Exciting Years Ahead

As we ponder the movies we will be watching and the music we will be listening to in the future, certain conclusions are inescapable. The literature of parking will increase dramatically and most movies will have a parking theme, at least in an underlying sense, especially where underground parking is concerned. This will not require as major an artistic shift as you might have thought. In the movies of earlier decades, people killed and fought and lied and cheated for gold or for sex. Now they will do it for parking.

Certain of the details will be different, of course. Actors who can parallel park will be in demand. Those who need diagonal parking will not do so well, although scripts may be rewritten to accommodate those with the biggest names. In some cases, stunt parkers may have to be hired.

Demographically, the movies of the new century will reflect the demographics of the population. They will be about older people, people of sixty and seventy, trying for dignity, trying for a parking place. Young people will be seen only in minor roles, portraying characters whose cars get in the way.

There will be dance crazes in the future, of course, as there always are. These will require people to move not at all rapidly. The information sector will keep track and let people know when crazes are old-hat and must be replaced by new ones.

The expression Old Hat will continue, for some reason.

Partly because of the continuing economic influence of Japan, karaoke will survive well into the new century and be modified to stay fresh and modern. One anticipated refinement is the introduction of political karaoke, envisioned as a hit in capital-city bars. In political karaoke, patrons are given a choice of political speeches to recite, which the tape machine accompanies with hearty applause – except for those rare and brooding souls who are deeply into boos. In more spacious bars, sports karaoke will be popular, with customers swinging their choice of golf club, while the machine broadcasts a videotape of an approach to the eighteenth green by Jack Nicklaus or another golfer selected by the customer.

In the country music of the future, people will be hurtin' from having to circle the block in the truck all the time.

The self-help book will become the major literary art form of the new century, and cutting-edge writers will continually discover new psychological burdens that readers will have to be taught to cast off, after first establishing where the blame for them lies. Parking dysfunctions will loom large. Some of them will be blamed on cars themselves; others will be traceable back to early automotive influences in the family.

Your Future Home: A Cineplex with a Back Yard

While many North Americans will venture out from time to time out of a sense of duty, a feeling that they owe it to the economy to try to find a parking place, most will prefer to entertain themselves and their families within the confines of their homes.

The trend toward specialization in cable channels will accelerate. There was an all-cartoon channel before the Nineties were out and the next decade will see further additions, such as the channel that looks like a tropical-fish tank. There will be a channel that shows hospital waiting-rooms and another devoted entirely to the monster movies of the Fifties and Sixties. People watching that can see tarantulas, locusts, and rabbits as big as apartment buildings, and remember the good old days. The Solitaire Channel will be a big hit.

Improving technologies will enable easier videotaping of such material and better home production techniques will allow the future family to preserve even more of its life, if any, for posterity. Videotaped funerals and divorces will join the videotaped wedding on the family shelves. If the trend to self-absorption that has characterized recent decades continues, people will want cameras in their own rooms, in order to get to know themselves much better. Important digestive functions may some day be recorded as a matter of routine, and the camera will certainly be rolling when Uncle Harry is thawed out after having been frozen since 1973.

The future, in case you had forgotten it, is the time when cryogenics, the art of deep-freezing people until there is a cure for what ails them, comes to fruition, as it were. The disease that laid low Uncle Harry having been cured, he can be thawed, treated, and live a normal life, at least theoretically. He will have to be eased back into society, of course, gently lectured on the sanctity of parking and why he can't go back to the farm without a tee-off time.

New questions of etiquette will challenge us in the future and perhaps none is so tricky as what to say to Uncle Harry when he thaws.

Thawing Uncle Harry: Dos and Don'ts

1. DO introduce yourself. Uncle Harry may remember who you are, but he has been sleeping for twenty years and you haven't.

2. DON'T say, "Jeez, you've got a cold handshake!"

The subject matter handled by the advice columnists of the future may seem a bit esoteric, but the tone will be familiar.

Q. When my Uncle Harry woke up after being frozen for twenty years, he immediately wanted to go to the office and check if there was any mail for him. We think that was rude of him and we also think he is displaying some of the same characteristics that got him into health trouble in the first place. How can we suggest to him politely that he go back to being frozen for a little bit longer?
A. It will not be easy. Remember the old saying" Once frozen, twice shy." In all likelihood, your uncle will not react well to the direct approach. Let him go to the office and try to find a place to park. When he returns, make sure the heat is turned up quite a lot.

Q. Owing to the failure of the education system, my daughter is unable to obtain employment in the parking sector and has had to settle for a job as vice-president of a television network. How will we explain this to the neighbours if they find out?
A. Not everybody can work in the parking sector. Many people are honourably employed doing work that, at least indirectly, keeps the parking sector going. Television, for example, lures people to stores through its advertising and many of those people need to park. Even if your daughter is involved in one of the less valuable areas, such as news, there is nothing to be ashamed about. Many people have gone from television news to useful work in parking lots.

Q. My friend and I recently formed a golf ball salvage company. It is called Mr. Water Hazard and we are quite confident of success. However, we are a bit uncertain about the etiquette of the business and would appreciate any tips you can pass along.
A. Diving for golf balls in golf course water hazards is still a fairly new occupation, but already certain rules of behaviour have been established. The most important of these is to turn off your air tank while people are putting.

Q. The videotapes I make of myself – my studying, my writing, my meditation, my yoga – are of the highest quality. Even the sound is good. The problem is that I can't get anybody to watch with me. Even members of my family want me to watch theirs with them. What's wrong with society today?
A. Stop bothering us. Can't you see we're busy? People have become excessively self-centred, is the problem, if you have to know.

Q. I have been reading old books and have come across references to an activity called "parties." In this activity, people left their homes and went to the homes of other people for eating and drinking and conversation and whatnot. Do you have any suggestions for reviving this activity now?
A. The key is to get people out of their homes, where they could be watching the Tropical Fish Network, swimming in the bathtub, or engaging in any number of wholesome, educational, and healthy activities, which they can videotape to watch later. Your only chance is to make it absolutely clear on your invitations that the party will be videotaped and that there will be entertainment, such as live tropical fish.

Q. I have been watching the Tropical Fish Network for several years and it has given me an idea – namely, why

not get a real tropical-fish tank with real tropical fish? This would provide me with some companionship and also allow me to watch another channel, such as the Scenery Channel. Has this been tried and are there any risks involved?

A. One of the reasons this has never been tried is that most people know enough not to expect companionship from tropical fish. They were never very affectionate to begin with and now that they are on television all the time they have taken to putting on airs. This makes tank maintenance a problem. It sounds as if you have some rather warped ideas: Maybe after watching the Scenery Channel, you will want to have real plants and trees around your house. Get a grip. This is the future, after all.

Outer Space: An Imperfect Solution to the Parking Problem

There has been lots of romance about space in the twentieth century, beginning with the first monkey, continuing through the Soviet cosmonauts and the first American on the moon. There were orbiting space shuttles and space labs, some excellent movies. With each successive flight, Earth's knowledge of outer space increased. The more we learned, the more we realized we would have to be crazy to go out there.

Among the disadvantages of outer-space life we will find the following:

1. It is dark.

2. It is cold.

3. There is, in almost all certainty, no life. And there are certainly no parties.

4. There is parking but no shopping, the exact reverse of the situation on earth.

5. The only thing to do, once you get there, is to come back.

6. Coming back is boring.

But you know that we will go out there. Wherever there is parking, modern man must go.

There will be two airlines in the future, owned by the Japanese companies Ford and Disney. They will do everything they can to make outer-space travel more inviting. They will offer free trips to those points on Earth that still have airports – Topeka, Kyoto, Barcelona, and Toronto Island. The results will not be encouraging. Early on in space passenger travel, the airlines will temporarily abandon their experiments with weightlessness after some difficult washroom incidents and the problem with the soup.

Dos and Don'ts of Weightless Flight

DO be cheerful, but that does not extend to putting a spring into your step. Putting a spring into your step is the same as putting the ceiling onto your head.

DON'T chew tobacco or partake of any activity that will encourage sneezing.

DO hang on tight to your partner if participating in amorous activity. It is irritating to first-class passengers to have naked people floating by during dinner.

After three-dimensional bingo is banned, Air Disney will attempt a bold experiment. "They call these things 'space ships,'" a Disney executive will say (in translation from the Japanese). "Why don't we make them more like ships?"

So Air Disney will, instituting deck tennis, shuffleboard, a captain's table, and passing out blankets to cover passengers' knees during afternoon tea. An orchestra will play and shipboard romances will be available for first-class passengers. Economy-class passengers will receive earphones, on which recordings of shipboard romances play on Channel 6.

The new service will be received well initially. In time, however, passengers will grow weary of being hit on the back of the head by deck-tennis rings. While the passengers selected to sit at the captain's table will be honoured, others will resent dressing for dinner during the short Jupiter-to-Mars hop and will be annoyed by the fact that the captain's table clogs the aisles and makes it impossible to get to the washrooms. Word of customer dissatisfaction will leak to the media, which will begin investigating and discover the lack of lifeboats. When passengers on the Kyoto-to-Venus run hear the orchestra playing "Nearer My God to Thee," it will all be over, although the bandleader will claim later that it had played "Chattanooga Choo-choo" and the song had been misquoted.

Once having arrived, no one will complain about the space stations themselves. They will have the full range of services – coffee machines, luggage carousels, video games with Smell-O-Matic, car rentals, plastic plants, and synthetic music. The unpopularity of space will derive from what happens after the visitor leaves the space station and looks for some sights to see.

Rocks are what the space visitor will see. A sea of rocks, broken occasionally by an island of dust. Not everyone will hate this – the International Federation of Rock and Dust Clubs will charter spacecraft annually for picture-taking excursions. But the consensus will be that space is best experienced on reruns of *Star Trek: The Generation After That*. Connoisseurs of the planets will point to differences in colour and texture in the dust of the different planets. Ordinary travellers will still prefer Earth, for the variety of its landscape, its choice of smoggy mountains, polluted lakes, and garbage-littered beaches.

For a time, it will be believed that there is life on Venus. Spacecraft will pick up lifelike noises, and telescope-mounted cameras will display oddly moving shadows that could be made by oddly moving creatures. There will be great excitement, cover stories in the news magazines, and a new approach taken by several supermarket tabloids, which discover, first, that Elvis is alive on Venus, second, that he is married, third, that his marriage is to a five-headed Venusian with blue nail polish, and fourth, that the Venusian, for some reason, only wears four hats.

Movie rights to the story of the Venus space expedition will be snapped up by the Japanese company Twentieth-Century Fox, the auction for press accreditation will be held, the T-shirts and bubblegum cards printed up. Then it will be discovered that the sounds and shadows were made by a made-for-Pay-TV movie that had bounced the wrong way off a satellite and escaped into space. After only a few weeks drifting through the void, it had lost all semblance of plot and only a hint of dramatic tension remained. The large press corps will dwindle, it being the consensus that no one wants to journey into space just to cover a movie. One critic will make the voyage and pronounce the movie "flawed."

There will be several other false alarms:

* A Japanese-owned Latvian space lab hears what it thinks is jazz coming from the vicinity of Mercury.

* A supermarket tabloid reports on a flock of geese spotted on Jupiter, inexplicably flying west.

* A rookie first baseman for the Chicago Cubs bats .628 over the first few weeks of the 2007 season and gives interviews saying he is from Saturn. It is soon discovered that he cannot hit a curveball. After his average drops to .168 it is learned that he is from Winnipeg.

Nevertheless, the time must eventually come. Real, live extraterrestrials will appear and there will be no question about it. We will know. They will have enough extra arms or legs, the right unearthly colour of skin. They will talk with little metallic pinging sounds like extraterrestrials did in 1950s movies when they came in peace and landed by the Washington Monument but we misunderstood them.

There will be no misunderstanding them this time. How

we treat them and how we are treated by them will depend to some extent on where we meet. Will it be on their turf or ours? They may land here, in which case we will probably try to make them welcome by lavishing upon them pizza and souvenirs. If it is on their turf, they will undoubtedly put on a traditional welcoming ceremony, which could be long and might resemble some of the dances you see now in basement clubs, only performed by blue people with five heads and four hats. Who knows?

Most likely, we will meet on neutral territory, in outer space. After first establishing that we are not going to shoot each other – not an easy task, because who knows, with extra-terrestrials, exactly what is a gun and what isn't – discussion will begin.

How To Have a Meaningful Conversation with an Extraterrestrial

1. Avoid the usual conversation openers. People from other planets are not likely to be following the National Hockey League. As for the weather, in outer space there is no weather. Or if there is weather, it is always the same.

2. Search for shared experiences. "So, the weather's the same as usual, eh," you could say, or: "Sure is dark out there." If you want to ask a leading question, you could try something like: "Have you had any air recently?"

3. No matter how attractive extraterrestrials may be, and no matter how long it's been since you had a date, avoid flirting. For one thing, you don't know which sex an extraterrestrial might be. There might be a choice of five or six, and you want to find out how they all work before committing yourself in any way. Better to be cautious, at least until you've watched a bit of their TV and can figure out who is who. A helpful hint: To identify the most attractive female extraterrestrial, look for the creature who is with the sheriff at the end of the movie.

4. Whip out your cellular. After showing them that it is not to eat, offer to let them phone home.

5. Avoid puns and wisecracks, which may not be understood. Something like "What's so extra about you?" may sound amusing to you, but is likely to be met by five blank expressions. Then you'll have to explain: "Well, see, we call people like you extraterrestrials, and the word 'extra' has another meaning, like in supermarkets soap is called 'extra-large' and so on, so you see, it was like a joke, sort of."

6. By all means, flatter an extraterrestrial on mastering our language. You don't need to mention that metallic pinging sound. Ask how they learned the language. Probably it was from a movie about a spacecraft landing at the Washington Monument.

But what if there is no discussion? This is where it gets tricky. We always assumed – it was always assumed in the movies – that we would be able to talk. Not only that, but we would be able to talk in English, which the extraterrestrials could manage well, despite the metallic pinging accent. That certainly was the way it would work out best for the main movie-going part of Earth's population, given our well-known aversion to subtitles. But what if the assumption is wrong?

The assumption rests on the notion that other civilizations in space are far more advanced than ours, so advanced that all they have to do is hear a language and their computers, or computer-like brains, can decipher it instantly and make it possible for all the inhabitants to speak it. Why we think that is difficult to know. Is it because we figure that no other society could be more primitive than ours? Do we imagine that the mere act of getting here from There demands such technological sophistication that language would be no problem?

Certainly, assuming that communication will be possible makes the creation of science fiction easier. But what if we are wrong? What if the extraterrestrials we finally encounter are even dumber than we are? Imagine them, clunking around the galaxy in some kind of wooden spaceship, all bound together with twine. They encounter us by accident (they are looking for Jupiter and don't have radar or anything). They have five heads and none of them are any good. They don't speak English or understand it. We try French, Chinese, Italian, Pig Latin, Valley Girl, Canadian – nothing works. They only speak Glack, and that not so well, as it turns out. We never bothered to learn Glack because we always counted on the extraterrestrials being the smart ones.

So there we are, the Glackians and us, frightened out of our wits, because we can't communicate and who knows what might be a weapon. They look at our ears and wonder if at any moment some explosive dart is going to come shooting out. We try gestures; we make peace signs and hold our hands out and smile. We pantomime wanting to know what their fax number is. They don't understand our gestures. They don't know what a smile is, not having movies. Their gestures of friendship, consisting of shuffling their hooves on the floor and twirling their antennae around their heads, are no more reassuring to us. They can't understand why we can't understand them. To them, their gestures and language are state-of-the-art. On the planet Glack, it is the Information Age.

Is this the way the world will end? It seems as likely as anything else: A bunch of one-headed people face-to-faces with a bunch of five-headed people, each side unable to communicate with the other. Tension mounts, distrust pervades. Finally, some hothead – it doesn't matter on which side – reaches for his phone . . .

OTHER TITLES FROM

⟦DOUGLAS GIBSON BOOKS⟧

PUBLISHED BY McCLELLAND & STEWART INC.

AT THE COTTAGE: A Fearless Look at Canada's Summer Obsession *by* Charles Gordon *illustrated by* Graham Pilsworth
This perennial best-selling book of gentle humour is "a delightful reminder of why none of us addicted to cottage life will ever give it up." *Hamilton Spectator*
Humour, 6 × 9, 224 pages, illustrations, trade paperback

BACK TALK: A Book for Bad Back Sufferers and Those Who Put Up With Them *by* Eric Nicol *illustrated by* Graham Pilsworth
This "little gem" (*Quill and Quire*) caused one reader – Mrs. E. Nicol – to write: "Laughing at this book cured my bad back. It's a miracle!"
Humour, 5½ × 8½, 136 pages, illustrations, trade paperback

THE ASTOUNDING LONG-LOST LETTERS OF DICKENS OF THE MOUNTED *edited by* Eric Nicol
These "letters" from Charles Dickens's son, a Mountie from 1874 to 1886, are "a glorious hoax … so cleverly crafted, so subtly hilarious." *Vancouver Sun*
Fiction, 4¼ × 7, 296 pages, paperback

FOR ART'S SAKE: A new novel *by* W.O. Mitchell
A respected art professor and his public-spirited friends decide to liberate great paintings from private collections. When the caper turns serious and the police are on their trail, it's the usual magical Mitchell mixture of tragedy and comedy.
Fiction, 6 × 9, 240 pages, hardcover

OVER FORTY IN BROKEN HILL: Unusual Encounters in the Australian Outback *by* Jack Hodgins
What's a nice Canadian guy doing in the midst of kangaroos, red deserts, sheepshearers, floods and tough Aussie bars? Just writing an unforgettable book, mate.
Travel, 5½ × 8½, 216 pages, trade paperback

WHO HAS SEEN THE WIND *by* W.O. Mitchell *illustrated by* William Kurelek
For the first time since 1947, this well-loved Canadian classic is presented in its full, unexpurgated edition, and is "gorgeously illustrated." *Calgary Herald*
Fiction, 8½ × 10, 320 pages, colour and black-and-white illustrations, hardcover

HUGH MACLENNAN'S BEST: An anthology *selected by* Douglas Gibson
This selection from all of the works of the witty essayist and famous novelist is "wonderful … It's refreshing to discover again MacLennan's formative influence on our national character." *Edmonton Journal*   *Anthology, 6 × 9, 352 pages, hardcover*